Road Vehicle
for
Model Railways

Ian Morton

Ian Allan
PUBLISHING

First published 2007

ISBN (10) 0 7110 3154 1
ISBN (13) 978 0 7110 3154 8

Published by Ian Allan Publishing

an imprint of Ian Allan Publishing Ltd, Hersham Surrey KT12 4RG.
Printed by Ian Allan Printing Ltd, Hersham, Surrey KT12 4RG.

Code: 0711/C

Visit the Ian Allan Publishing web site at: www.ianallanpublishing.com

Cover:
A Corgi Burlingham Seagul in Barton livery bound for Skegness, has just crossed over Ankle Bend level crossing on Chris Nevard's '00' gauge Combwich model railway layout. The delapidated Austin 'Devon' see to the right is a customised vehicle from the Classix diecast range.
Photo: Chris Nevard

Title page:
Road vehicles can make interesting loads for wagons. The Airfix/Dapol JCB model on a Lowmac is a common sight on many model railways, but rarely as well portrayed as this. The JCB has been lightly weathered, the rear arm removed for transit and the whole lot secured in place.
Photo: Kier Hardy

Contents

Preface   **4**

CHAPTER **1**   **Introduction**   **5**

CHAPTER **2**   **Period, type and quantity**   **11**

CHAPTER **3**   **Roads, signs and registration plates**   **23**

CHAPTER **4**   **Building road vehicles**   **33**

CHAPTER **5**   **Detailing**   **44**

CHAPTER **6**   **Making them move**   **63**

Appendices:

     UK Manufacturers and Suppliers   73

     Periodicals, Clubs and Societies   74

     Selective 4 mm Scale Model Listing   75

Preface

Model road vehicles are one of the Cinderellas of railway modelling. Most people seem to begrudge spending time, effort or money on something that is not actually directly part of the railway. This is a shame as correctly modelled vehicles and street scenes can not only add to the overall impression of reality but can help to define the location and time of a modelled scene, even without a train in sight.

Whilst in some ways it has never been easier to obtain reasonable scale models of vehicles to suit most periods, the availability of relatively cheap die-cast models that are roughly the right size has, to some extent, had a negative effect. Bad vehicles do more to destroy the atmosphere that is created by the otherwise careful observation and modelling of a scene than no vehicles at all.

In writing this volume I hope to demonstrate that with relatively little work and expense it is possible to elevate the road vehicles on your layout to a state where they help, rather than hinder, the realism of the scene that you are trying to portray.

Vehicle modelling can be addictive, especially given the speed with which some models can be completed and the extra life that they bring to the modelled scene.

Finally I should like to thank those who have provided photographs and information, and my family for tolerating my many hours putting this book together.

Happy modelling.

Ian Morton

Chapter 1: Introduction

A siding and some hard-standing give ample possibilities for adding interesting traffic to your model railway. Here a selection of military vehicles immediately identify this facility as one used by the Ministry of Defence, giving scope for all manner of traffic from nondescript crates in vans through to armoured cars on Warflats.

I have been reading model railway magazines and attending exhibitions for more years than I care to admit to and despite the staggering advances that have been made in the quality of models that are available and the layouts that are produced, one area seems to have seen little change in that time; road vehicles and street scenes. It is as though a form of blindness afflicts most railway modellers when they look beyond the railway fence. All of a sudden they become blind to scale, period and detail. It is a malaise that seems as likely to strike the P4 modeller as the ready-to-run OO operator. It is as if anything that is not a train, or directly related to them, should be dealt with as quickly and cheaply as possible. There are honourable exceptions to this generalisation, but even some celebrated layouts fall into the trap. This is a great shame as not only can well modelled roads and vehicles help locate a layout in both time and place but ill-suited ones can undo all the work put in elsewhere and ruin any illusion of reality.

Today much railway equipment is moved by road, but in the 1970s it was an unusual event which required specialist hauliers and police escorts. Here is Duke of Gloucester on its way to a new life in preservation.
Photo: Author's collection

Agricultural vehicles can make an interesting addition to a lineside field. The combine harvester, an old Matchbox model, is under scale but, in this case, this is an advantage as an accurate model would overwhelm the scene.

It looks like the demolition crew are moving in to deal with this old building on Kier Hardy's Wibdenshaw layout.
Photo: Kier Hardy

A scene that is sadly typical of many model railways. Inaccurate, out of scale toys destroy any illusion of reality.

Fortunately there is a vast range of models that can be used to provide road vehicles for virtually any UK outline model railway. The amount of work needed to make reasonable representations of the prototype out of them varies, as does the cost, but the effort and expense involved is amply rewarded in the overall increase in the realism of your modelled scenes. In many cases the dictum 'less is more' applies as a small number of well detailed in-period vehicles will achieve far more than a larger number of 'out-of-the-box' items.

Road vehicles can be used to add life and purpose to a model. Large stations need bus stops and taxi ranks, goods yards need lorries to load or unload, streets of shops need parked cars for the customers and vans for deliveries, farms need tractors, the list is endless. Your selection of vehicles can also help to convey more subtle messages. The cars in an affluent area will be different to those in a slum. Different types of lorry are used for different freights. The buses for services down country lanes will often be different to those that ply their trade in the heart of a city. Your choice of vehicles will help people to build up a picture of the area that you are trying to portray.

The combination of closed level crossing gates and a Scammell Scarab gently manoeuvring out of some industrial premises have brought all traffic to a halt on this part of Ken Johnson's Kenborough layout.

Kier Hardy's Wibdenshaw is obviously a major transport hub as evidenced by the bus services that call at the station. The buses also help to place the station in West Yorkshire in the 1970s.
Photo: Kier Hardy

Virtually anywhere that rail-borne freight is loaded or unloaded needs vehicular access. Here a Ford lorry hides behind a class 03 shunting at Wibdenshaw's goods yard.
Photo: Kier Hardy

Road vehicles don't have to be confined to roads. Here an old coach is partially sheeted up, quietly decaying, awaiting preservation. This was produced from an EFE die-cast model.

A selection of out of scale, out of period and generally unprepossessing road vehicles add nothing to this scene.

The addition of some road markings, a road sign and a set of detailed, scale vehicles transforms the scene. There is more that could be done, such as adding street lights, but it is a big improvement over the previous photo.

There is also the thorny question of the static landscape that our model trains run through. Whilst the trains move, everything else from buses to dogs remains frozen in place, as though some enemy of Doctor Who had zapped the area with some strange ray. Whilst you can make your road vehicles move (see chapter 6) you still need to consider the people. Moving vehicles need drivers (just like moving trains – you do have drivers in your locomotives, don't you?). If you don't have moving vehicles then it is best to use your vehicles in stationary positions. Cars parked, lorries being loaded, buses at stops and so on.

Apart from the increased visual appeal that well modelled road vehicles will bring to your layout, there are other advantages to spending a bit of time bringing them up to scratch. You can quite quickly complete small cameo scenes that add points of interest to your layout, perhaps highlighting a feature that you are proud of – or drawing attention away from something that you aren't. More importantly you can use vehicle projects to learn new skills and practice on models that are usually cheaper and less important than your locomotives and rolling stock. If you learn to paint, decal, cut, fill, assemble and detail on your road vehicles you will build the skill and confidence to tackle bigger, more complex jobs.

You can find inspiration in many places. If you model the current railway scene then you only need to model what you see on the roads every day. If you model a historical period, then referring to archive photographs will open up a window on a different world. Many railway photographs include the surrounding landscape with cars, roads and street furniture. In addition, there are books of old photographs of many areas which can provide a wealth of information and the internet is another great resource for locating images to serve as inspiration.

Right, that's enough preamble, let's get down to business ...

Chapter 2: Period, type and quantity

Careful selection of the road vehicles used on your layout can convey a lot of information about the period and location, even when there are no trains in sight. On the other hand, getting your road vehicles wrong can destroy the illusion that you are trying to create.

A cynical definition of a pedestrian is 'someone who has found a place to park their car'. A street full of parked cars hints that this is a busy area despite the lack of moving traffic.
Photo: Kier Hardy

This photo of London's Parliament Square in the 1950s shows how little traffic there could be, even in the centre of the capital. Note the almost total lack of signs and road markings.
Photo: Author's collection

This current-day scene in Shrewsbury contrasts with Parliament Square. There is more traffic, more road markings and signs.

Even as recently as the 1960s British roads were relatively empty with few vehicles on them. Main roads tended to go through towns rather than round them, there were fewer signs and road markings and many people used bicycles and public transport rather than own a car. In the 1960s and 1970s the number of private cars increased dramatically. This was combined with a switch from rail to road for much freight and there was a road-building boom with many bypasses being built to take the heavy traffic out of towns and villages.

In recent years we have seen the growth of industrial estates and retail parks on the edge of towns and these have become major traffic destinations – in many cases more so than the old town centre. In many places car ownership is now an essential part of everyday life. With the proliferation of traffic we now have more road signs and measures such as speed humps, speed cameras and bus lanes that use specially coloured tarmac.

For layouts set even as little as ten years ago it is necessary to refer to photographs to see just how much has changed. A good photograph will not only help with the road and vehicles but also other scenic details such as the clothing styles, shop fronts and building details for the period in question.

There is a large number of road vehicles available to the modeller in 4mm scale but, in many cases, the more common vehicles seen every day are in the minority compared to the expensive and exotic types. The rest of this chapter is devoted to a quick run-down of various of the model ranges that may be of use when making road vehicles.

Base Toys

The Base Toys range is not only correctly scaled for 4mm scale but is also 'modeller friendly' as the vehicles can easily be taken apart so that you can mix and match the parts if required. This photo shows a Ford D series flatbed (left) and a Leyland 'LAD' cabbed 6-wheel box van. The cabs were originally the other way around, but a few minutes' work with a screwdriver soon changed that.

This range consists of 4mm scale lorries. The models are built from interchangeable components that allow you to mix and match and come in plain paint schemes allowing the modeller to finish them to suit their own needs. At the time of writing there are eight different cab styles in the range: 1950s Albion Chieftain; late 50s/early 60s AEC Mercury; late 1940s Leyland Beaver; mid-50s Leyland 'Mouth Organ'; early 50s Leyland Comet; late 50s/early 60s LAD (Leyland/Albion/Dodge); late 60s/early 70s Ford D and late 50s/early 60s Thames Trader. The body styles available are a flatbed, dropside, tanker, four- and six-wheel box vans.

Bus Kits

There are a number of small manufacturers who produce 4mm scale model bus kits in both metal and resin. The resin kits are usually simple to build, comprising a one- or two-piece bodyshell, chassis with seating cast in place and few extra pieces. The metal kits are usually more complex, being cast in white metal or pewter and consist of sides, front and rear panels, roof, chassis, seating and other parts.

There are a number of ranges of kits for buses which can help to provide just the right type of vehicle for your layout's chosen location and period. From left to right: Midland Red S17 in Midland Red livery with a Shropshire destination blind suitable for the 1960s; Thames Valley Bristol SC suitable for Maidenhead–Marlow area, again in the 1960s; Badgerline Iveco minibus, suitable for Somerset in the early 1990s.

The range of kits available does change continuously, as most kits are produced in limited batches and once the batch has been sold the kit may not be produced again for a long while – if at all. Once you have identified a kit as being suitable for your layout you should buy it while you can. If you wait until you are ready to build it then the chances are that it will no longer be available.

In other scales the number of kits available is severely limited, as are supporting items such as fleet name decals.

A selection of bus kit manufacturers are listed in Appendix A along with details of the Model Bus Federation. This club is the best way to keep abreast of what kits are being planned and sold.

Cararama

Whilst most of the Cararama range is too large for use with 4mm scale quite a few are near enough for most people's purposes. Whilst the range does include some exotic machines there are also some useful everyday vehicles such as the ones illustrated here.

Very popular with railway modellers due to their ready availability and modest price, unfortunately many of the vehicles produced in the Cararama range are much too large for use with 4mm scale model railways. Whilst the boxes claim that they are all 1/72nd scale the actual scales vary widely from model to model. Those that are close to 4mm scale make an ideal basis for detailing and the wheels are useful for detailing other models. A selection of the available models, along with their actual scale, is listed in Appendix C.

Car Kits

There is a limited range of kits for cars, chiefly in 4mm scale. Most are produced in white metal or pewter although some come with resin bodies.

The available kits fall into two camps, those that come with a single-piece bodyshell and those that come with individual parts for bonnet, sides, roof, etc...

In most cases availability of the kit ranges is consistent so it is possible to buy them on an 'as required' basis. A selection of manufacturers is listed in Appendix A.

Classix

A range of die-cast lorries, cars and vans specifically produced for use with 4mm scale model railways. The range is aimed at the 1940s/50s era.

Corgi/Lledo Trackside

This range consists of various lorries and, a recent addition, vans and cars. A range of eras are covered up to the early/mid-1970s. Whilst the detailing is on the crude side they can produce fine models with a little care and attention.

Each combination of vehicle and livery is produced as a limited edition, so if you want a particular version you should get it when you see it.

EFE (Exclusive First Editions)

EFE produce a range of die-cast model buses, plus some lorries and sports cars, in 4mm scale. Each model is produced as a limited run and the livery/model combinations are not usually repeated. The models produced range from the 1920s to the present day and cover all areas of the country.

You should buy any models that are suitable for your needs as soon as they are released to be sure of obtaining them. Older models can be found at toy fairs, on eBay and by diligent scouring of retailers for old or second-hand stock.

EFE produce each model as a limited run, so if you miss it when released you will have to search toy fairs, eBay and retailers to fulfil your requirements. Left to right: London Transport STL; AEC Ergo cab articulated lorry – Tesco; NBC Midland Red Leyland National – Lancer MAP identity.

Lorry Kits

There is a reasonable variety of kits for lorries, chiefly in 4mm scale. Most are produced in white metal or pewter although some come with resin bodies.

In most cases availability of the kit ranges is consistent so it is possible to buy them on an 'as required' basis. A selection of manufacturers is listed in Appendix A.

Matchbox and Other Toy Cars

The battered Matchbox model has for many years been the standard fare of many model railways. A small number of such vehicles are, with some work, suitable for use, but the vast majority are not. The cars are, by and large, too big for 4mm scale and too small for 7mm, whilst the lorries are too small for 4mm scale and too large for 2mm. A guide to the models that are suitable for 4mm scale is included in Appendix A.

This Ford Zephyr started life as a Matchbox model. It has been repainted and had new wheels fitted along with wing mirrors, windscreen wipers and registration plates.

Minix

This range of plastic vehicles was produced by Triang in the 1960s and is ideal for a layout based in the 1960s and early 1970s. Whilst the models are basic, they are still readily available on the secondhand market and, on the whole, portray common types. Some of the models are easier to obtain than others, the Austin A60, Simca, Vauxhall Cresta and Vauxhall Victor being the hardest to find.

The range included:

Austin 1800 Mk.I, Austin A60, Ford Anglia Mk.3, Ford Corsair, Hillman Imp Mk.I, Hillman Minx Series V/VI, Morris 1100 Mk.I, Simca 1300, Sunbeam Alpine Series IV/V, Triumph 2000 Mk.II, Vauxhall Cresta Estate, Vauxhall Victor 101, Vauxhall Viva HA saloon and a Ford Thames 15 cwt van.

OOC (Original Omnibus Company)

OOC produce a range of die-cast model buses in 4mm scale. Each model is produced as a limited run and the livery/model combinations are not usually repeated. The models produced range from the 1940s to the present day and cover all areas of the country.

You should buy any models that are suitable for your needs as soon as they are released to be sure of obtaining them. Older models can be found at toy fairs, on eBay and by diligent scouring of retailers for old or second-hand stock.

No 1960s or early 1970s layout can afford to be without a good helping of Minix models. With a variety of mundane motor cars from the period they are just what is needed to make realistic street scenes.

OOC produce each model as a limited run, so if you miss it when released you will have to search toy fairs, eBay and retailers to fulfil your requirements. Left to right: Midland Red D9 from the 1960s and Metroline low-floor Dennis Dart from more recent times.

Oxford Diecast

Oxford Diecast has recently started to produce a range of die-cast model vehicles in 4mm scale. Each model will be produced as a limited run, so it is best to get any models that you need when they appear.

One of the first Oxford Diecast 4mm scale vans was this Morris Minor in Royal Mail livery. With a little work it can be made into an excellent model.

Specialist Vehicles

Specialist vehicles, such as breakdown trucks, fire engines, fairground and military vehicles have proved to be of far more interest to kit manufacturers than the more mundane vehicles suited to recreating everyday traffic. However, where a special vehicle is needed for a particular scene it is quite possible that a suitable kit may be located.

Die-cast ranges also find emergency service vehicles, such as police vehicles and ambulances, appealing, but more often than not they are poor generic representations rather than specific models.

Van Kits

There is a limited range of kits for vans and similar vehicles, such as pick-ups and crew buses, chiefly in 4mm scale. Most are produced in white metal or pewter although some in 2mm scale come as single-piece resin castings.

A selection of 4mm scale small commercials. From left to right: the archetypical Ford Transit, in crew bus guise; the Commer PB – much loved by the Post Office for mail and telephone work; a more recent incarnation of the Transit, this time in pick-up form.

The available kits fall into two camps, those that come with a single-piece bodyshell and those that come with individual parts for bonnet, sides, roof, etc.

In most cases availability of the kit ranges is consistent so it is possible to buy them on an 'as required' basis. A selection of manufacturers is listed in Appendix A.

Unexpected Finds

Never pass up the opportunity to look at the toys in pound shops and other outlets. You may just drop lucky and find something really useful. Always carry a size guide in your wallet so that you can check any vehicles you find for suitability. This selection came from a variety of places ranging from Cadbury World to a seaside gift shop, and all are suitable for use on 4mm scale layouts.

Even key rings can provide suitable vehicles. In the past I have seen Routemaster buses suitable for 'N' scale and FX4 taxis that could pass on 'OO' layouts. This key ring was sold in Marks & Spencer for the Christmas market and used a Cararama model. There was also Inspector Morse's Jaguar, but this was to 'HO' scale.

Keep your eyes open as you can sometimes find suitable model vehicles in the most unlikely places. In the past year I have found a Lledo Volvo articulated lorry at Cadbury World, a car transporter with four Cararama cars in Woolworths, a plastic coach in a seaside gift shop, various Cararama models in pound shops and a Reliant 3-wheeler attached to a key ring in Marks & Spencer.

If you carry a suitable size template in your wallet you can soon establish if a likely looking candidate is suitable for purchase. Don't forget that cheap vehicles, even of the wrong period, can sometimes provide parts to detail and convert other models. As an example the Cararama vehicles purchased at £1 each provided me with wheels, steering wheels and interior parts for a number of Minix cars.

A closer view of the Marks & Spencer key ring reveals that whilst it was designed to cash in on the popularity of the BBC series *Only Fools and Horses* it also happened to be a nicely detailed Reliant 3-wheel van. Removal of the key ring and roof rack followed by a repaint produces a model that looks right at home in a late 60s to mid-70s period scene.

Whilst sold as a toy at Cadbury World, this Lledo lorry is just right for a modern 4mm scale truck. With suitable detailing it can be converted from a toy into a useful model.

The Lledo lorry has been used as a promotional model for a number of companies and can often be found second-hand on eBay in liveries such as Tesco and Royal Mail which are ideal for the modern-day scene. It lends itself to detailing and repainting to recreate the many large trucks to be found servicing today's shops and industries.

This plastic coach, marketed under the Teamsters' label, was found in a seaside gift shop and is representative of many modern-day coach designs. With a small amount of work it can be turned into a quite convincing model.

Charity shops and seaside gift shops can often provide interesting finds. A typical modern coach, in the Teamsters range, suitable for 4mm scale was widely available a while back and recently I spotted a single deck bus in the same range that had potential.

Even high street stores can prove to be useful sources. Woolworths sometimes have suitable vehicles in their Chad Valley range, such as the Cararama-produced car transporter illustrated, and Wilkinsons have been known to have die-cast models in their toy section too.

This set was purchased from Woolworths. Sold under their Chad Valley label, it was produced by Cararama. It proved to be more economical than purchasing the individual cars at normal retail prices.

Road vehicles can be used to make little scenes, such as this National Express coach loading passengers at St Ives.

Life in a Northern town. Someone is doing very well for themselves, as the brand-new Lotus demonstrates. Meanwhile other residents make do with more mundane motors. This is a scene on the Manchester Model Railway Society's Dewsbury Midland layout. The Lotus is a Cararama model, whilst the other cars are TPM resin kits.
Photo: Andy York
www.rmweb.co.uk

Road/rail trans-shipment on modern railways often needs nothing more complex than some hard-standing alongside a siding. Here the Hiab crane on the lorry is being used to load the timber wagon. The logs on the ground must have been left on a previous journey, prior to the arrival of the wagon. Note that the lorry has wing mirrors, tail lights and registration plates.

Chapter 3: Roads, signs and registration plates

Roads

Road vehicles, road markings and street furniture such as road signs and street lights combine to make a believable scene on the road bridge over the station throat at Wibdenshaw.
Photo: Kier Hardy

Conventional wisdom has it that model roads should be black and flat. A moment looking out of your window should dispel any lingering notion you may have that real roads actually look like that. Roads are grey – the shade varies but is normally nearer to a mid-grey than black, and even a road that doesn't go up or down hill curves down from the centre to the gutters on either side. This is called the camber and is there to make water drain to the sides. There are a number of ways to put a camber on a model road. The one that you choose will depend on the complexity of the road layout and personal preference. Whatever you do, don't be tempted to use black flock powder or wet and dry paper – no matter how much you try they will never produce a convincing result.

For a straight length of road you can use card between 1mm and 2mm thick. The road surface is a layer of card glued along the edges (gutters) and supported by packing in the middle. If you really want to show the camber off, park a double-deck bus alongside the pavement. The road illustrated on p.24 is 136mm wide with 3mm of packing in the middle.

Not all roads are flat as this bumpy stretch shows. In order not to obstruct traffic on this busy road the police car has been illegally parked half on the pavement. The rear of the bus is a little mucky, all helping to make an interesting scene.
Photo: Kier Hardy

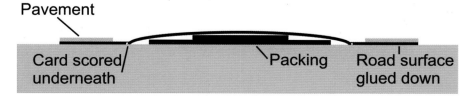

Pavement

Card scored underneath   Packing   Road surface glued down

Real roads are cambered, that is they are higher in the middle than at the sides. With a straight stretch of road you can reproduce this by packing up the centre of the road. The double-deck bus on the right shows the effect that camber has on tall vehicles at the side of the road.

The most realistic way to represent tarmac on card or other smooth surfaces is to paint a thick coat of dark grey paint onto the road, sift baby powder onto the paint through a tea strainer and then gently pat it down. There should be enough baby powder so that the paint does not soak through to the top. Once the paint is dry shake the excess powder off and blow off any that is reluctant to move. You should be left with a good representation of a tarmac road. Any areas that need further attention can be resurfaced, just like the real thing. Sometimes you even get realistic potholes where some of the baby powder has come away.

An alternative method to make a tarmac covering on a smooth surface is to use the texture sheets created by Scalescenes. These are computer files that you print yourself onto good quality paper, then cut out and stick down. Whilst the sheets come with various road markings, potholes and even some signs and bollards, they are largely limited to straight roads and junctions. The other limitation is that as you print onto A4 sheets you will need to cut and match a number of them even for a small road scene. One tip to get a near invisible join is to overlap sheets where they join and cut through them both. Provided you use a sharp blade the cut edges should align perfectly.

Template for road camber (not to scale).

For more complex road layouts with curves and junctions, if you want a camber then the best way is to build the road up from stiff plaster. You will need to cut a former, half a road wide from plastic sheet. To form the camber simply drag the former along the plaster, stopping frequently to remove the excess. Keeping the former wet will stop it dragging plaster away that should be staying put. It is a good idea to mix some grey paint in with the plaster; that way, if the road gets chipped you won't get small areas of bright white plaster showing through.

Of course, even today, not all roads are tarmac. There is a wide variety of surfaces and styles: concrete, gravel, mud and cobblestones to name a few. Concrete can be represented by painting with very fine pencil lines to indicate the joins between the sections. Gravel drives can be simulated using very fine railway ballast. Mud is best created using brown tinted plaster, along with some suitable grass to go in the centre of the track. Whilst you can purchase plastic sheets of moulded cobblestones, a better effect can be obtained by scribing them into plaster. This is, however, very time consuming.

Before we move on to pavements we need to consider the ironwork that can be found in roads. Along the gutter you will find drains and in the road itself there are manhole covers. The Scalescenes road surface set includes various drains and covers that can be printed, cut out and stuck down. Alternatively, etched items are available from both Langley Miniature Models and Taylor Precision Models.

Pavements

On model railways most pavements are modelled as paving slabs. There are a number of options for representing these including printed sheets, plastic sheet, individual card paving stones and plaster mouldings.

Printed papers, available from Scalescenes and Superquick need to be mounted on thick card. Whilst they are quick and easy for straight, narrow runs of paving they need careful work if you need wider sections or awkward shapes.

Plastic sheet, available in the Slaters and Wills ranges, is more amenable to awkward shapes but you do need to create your own kerb from plastic strip and, of course, paint the finished pavement. The thin embossed sheets in the Slaters range need to be mounted on thicker styrene sheets or card to bring them up to a reasonable thickness.

Metcalfe Models produce some pre-cut self-adhesive card paving stones. These come complete with suitable kerbs and provide a great deal of flexibility in creating paved areas. Depending on personal taste and prototype you may wish to colour the stones once laid.

Townstreet models provide plaster-cast paving sections to complement their range of buildings. Whilst they suffer from the same lack of flexibility as the printed sheets, the plaster does take paint well and a highly realistic finish can be achieved using these items.

Many real pavements are tarmaced and these can be produced using the same method as the road that they are alongside.

Road Signs and Markings

Road signs can help place your layout both in time and geographically. Prior to the early 1970s signs were not so prolific and to a different design to those in use today. Whilst you can purchase signs that give orders and information, such as 'Give Way', '30' and 'School', direction signs will need to be created specially for your model. Fortunately, with the aid of a home computer this is not a daunting task. Road signs use a special font, which can be downloaded from the internet, and have design rules which, you've guessed it, can be downloaded too. Most drawing or word-processing programs have sufficient facilities to enable you to produce direction signs tailored to your layout.

These signs were produced on a home computer using a drawing program. They are destined for the author's 'Redhill' layout.

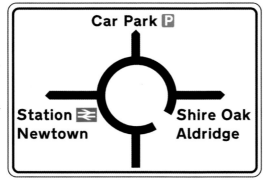

If you don't have access to the internet then a copy of the Highway Code for the era in which your model is set is a really useful acquisition. This will give pictures of the signs and road markings in use at the time. For those with internet access the current Highway Code can be viewed on-line, complete with illustrations of current signs and road markings at www.highwaycode.gov.uk/signs_index.htm. The CBRD website, www.cbrd.co.uk, has much interesting information on roads and road signs, along with the correct Transport fonts which can be downloaded to your computer from www.cbrd.co.uk/media/fonts/ which also includes the older font used for signs prior to 1964. To create realistic signs you should either copy a real sign or refer to the official standards which can be found at www.dft.gov.uk/pgr/roads/tss/tsmanual/, chapter 7 being the most relevant section for our needs.

Virtually every urban street has a name displayed either on a free-standing sign or plate attached to a building. These come in a huge variety of shapes and styles. As with direction signs they are ideal candidates for production on a home computer, giving you a unique set of streets; alternatively, printed sheets of names are available in the Tiny Signs range.

Mandatory and information signs, such as speed restrictions and hazards, are available from a number of suppliers. You can, of course, use the images from the Highway Code to produce your own signs if you wish. The current pictogram-style signs started to appear in the early 1970s. Before this time signs included more words and different symbols. The changeover to the new signs took many years and, even today, the occasional early sign can be spotted in odd locations. Both modern and older signs are included in the ranges produced by Hornby, Roger Smith and Tiny Signs. Don't forget that there used to be far fewer signs than there are now.

Road markings are difficult to reproduce and badly painted markings will not produce a convincing model. Some rub-down transfer sheets are available from European manufacturers, but these are for German road markings and so are of limited use to UK modellers. Fortunately, Roger Smith provides stick-on 4mm scale road markings in both white and yellow.

Traffic Lights and Street Lights

Unless your road vehicles actually move (see chapter 6) there is little point in having operating traffic lights. Dummy lights are available from both Langley Models and Hornby in their Skaledale range.

Pedestrian crossings come in two versions, the traditional zebra crossing, which was first introduced in 1951 and the traffic-controlling Pelican which was introduced in 1969. The two components of the zebra crossing are the road markings, available in 4mm scale in the Roger Smith range, and the flashing Belisha beacons mounted on the pavement. Dummy beacons can be found in the Langley and Hornby Skaledale range whilst working ones can be obtained from Express Models. There is, as far as I know, no model of a Pelican crossing available at the time of writing, but it should be possible to modify a set of traffic lights to suit.

Street lights vary in size and style but are a must in any urban setting. Dummy street lamps appear in a number of ranges and it is also possible to obtain working lamps, although these tend to become expensive when you need to equip a reasonable length of road. If you are tempted to fit working street lamps, don't forget that you will also need to fit lighting to buildings and other scenic features on your layout.

Registration Plates

The story of car registration plates is incredibly complex. This is a brief summary for the UK mainland and should suffice for most modellers' purposes. Whilst registration plates can easily be produced on a home computer, or purchased from decal suppliers such as Fox Transfers, Mabex and Modelmaster, getting a registration that fits your model layout is a little harder.

Car registrations have been with us since 1903. The first registration plates were white or silver characters on a black background and were made up of one letter and number. The very first, A 1, was issued by London Council. As more registrations were issued the format changed to two letters followed by up to four numbers (AB 1234). By the mid-1930s some areas had exhausted their two letter/four digit combinations and moved on to three letter/three digit combinations (ABC 123). Again some areas exhausted these combinations earlier than others and in the mid-1950s a new series of three digit/three letter combinations (123 ABC) was introduced.

Sometime between 1963 and 1965, depending on the area, all new registrations changed to a new format with three letters, three digits and a letter suffix (ABC 123D). The suffix indicated the year in which the vehicle was registered as follows:

A	Feb 63 to Dec 63	M	Aug 73 to Jul 74
B	Jan 64 to Dec 64	N	Aug 74 to Jul 75
C	Jan 65 to Dec 65	P	Aug 75 to Jul 76
D	Jan 66 to Dec 66	R	Aug 76 to Jul 77
E	Jan 67 to Jul 67	S	Aug 77 to Jul 78
F	Aug 67 to Jul 68	T	Aug 78 to Jul 79
G	Aug 68 to Jul 69	V	Aug 79 to Jul 80
H	Aug 69 to Jul 70	W	Aug 80 to Jul 81
J	Aug 70 to Jul 71	X	Aug 81 to Jul 82
K	Aug 71 to Jul 72	Y	Aug 82 to Jul 83
L	Aug 72 to Jul 73		

In 1973 number plates were changed to a reflective design with black characters on a white background at the front and black on yellow at the rear. These were designed so that unlit vehicles were easier to see at night. The new-style plates were only required on new vehicles; fitting them on older vehicles was voluntary and was fairly rare.

In 1983 there was another change when the suffix series of registrations was replaced by a prefix series. These had the age prefix, three numbers and then three letters (A123 BCD) as follows:

A	Aug 83 to Jul 84	M	Aug 94 to Jul 95
B	Aug 84 to Jul 85	N	Aug 95 to Jul 96
C	Aug 85 to Jul 86	P	Aug 96 to Jul 97
D	Aug 86 to Jul 87	R	Aug 97 to Jul 98
E	Aug 87 to Jul 88	S	Aug 98 to Feb 99
F	Aug 88 to Jul 89	T	Mar 99 to Jul 99
G	Aug 89 to Jul 90	V	Aug 99 to Feb 2000
H	Aug 90 to Jul 91	W	Mar 2000 to Jul 2000
J	Aug 91 to Jul 92	X	Aug 2000 to Feb 2001
K	Aug 92 to Jul 93	Y	Mar 2001 to Jul 2001
L	Aug 93 to Jul 94		

Between 1963 and 2001 each area was allocated a number of registration series. These two letter combinations were the second and third letters of the three letter group. Thus APS 123 would have been issued in Aberdeen (PS), RDA 234H in Birmingham (DA) and M345 TAA in Bournemouth (AA). The prefix Q was introduced in 1983 for cars of uncertain age (Q123 ABC).

Aberdeen	PS, RS, SA, SE, SO, SS
Birmingham	DA, JW, OA, OB, OC, OE, OF, OG, OH, OJ, OK, OL, OM, ON, OP, OV, OX, UK, VP
Bournemouth	AA, CG, EL, FX, HO, JT, LJ, PR, RU
Brighton	AP, CD, DY, FG, HC, JK, NJ, PN, UF, WV, YJ
Bristol	AE, EU, FB, HT, HU, HW, HY, OU, TC, WS
Cardiff	AX, BO, DW, HB, KG, NY, TG, TX, UH, WO, AO, HH, RM
Chelmsford	AR, EV, HJ, HK, JN, NO, OO, PU, TW, VW, VX, WC
Chester	CA, DM, FM, LG, MA, MB, TU
Coventry	AC, DU, HP, KV, RW, VC, WK
Dudley	DH, EA, FD, FK, HA, NX, UE, WD
Dundee	ES, SL, SN, SP, SR, TS
Edinburgh	FS, KS, LS, MS, SC, SF, SG, SH, SX
Exeter	CO, DR, DV, FJ, JY, OD, TA, TK, TT, UN, UO
Glasgow	CS, DS, GA, GB, GD, GE, GG, HS, NS, OS, SB, SD, SJ, SM, SU, SW, US, YS
Gloucester	AD, CJ, DD, DF, DG, FH, FO, VJ
Guildford	PA, PB, PC, PD, PE, PF, PG, PH, PJ, PK, PL, PM
Haverfordwest	BX, DE, EJ
Huddersfield	CP, CX, HD, JX, VH
Hull	AG, AT, KH, RH
Inverness	AS, BS, JS, SK, ST
Ipswich	BJ, DX, GV, PV, RT
Leeds	BT, DN, NW, UA, UB, UG, UM, VY, WR, WT, WU, WW, WX, WY, YG
Leicester	AY, BC, FP, JF, JU, NR, RY, UT
Lincoln	BE, CT, DO, EE, FE, FU, FW, JL, JV, TL, VL
Liverpool	BG, CM, DJ, ED, EK, EM, FY, HF, JP, KA, KB, KC, KD, KF, LV, TB, TJ, WM
London (Central)	HM, HV, HX, JD, UC, UL, UU, UV, UW, YE, YF, YH, YK, YL, YM, YN, YO, YP, YR, YT, YU, YV, YW, YX, YY
London NE	MC, MD, ME, MF, MG, MH, MK, ML, MM, MP, MT, MU
London NW	BY, LA, LB, LC, LD, LE, LF, LH, LK, LL, LM, LN, LO, LP, LR, LT, LU, LW, LX, LY, OY, RK
London SE	GU, GW, GX, GY, MV, MX, MY
London SW	GC, GF, GH, GJ, GK, GN, GO, GP, GT
Luton	BH, BM, GS, KX, MJ, NK, NM, PP, RO, TM, UR, VS
Maidstone	FN, JG, JJ, KE, KJ, KK, KL, KM, KN, KO, KP, KR, KT, VB
Manchester	BA, BN, BU, CB, DB, DK, EN, JA, NA, NB, NC, ND, NE, NF, RJ, TD, TE, VM, VR, VU, WH
Middlesbrough	AJ, DC, EF, HN, PY, VN

Newcastle upon Tyne	BB, BR, CN, CU, FT, GR, JR, NL, PT, RG, TN, TY, UP, VK
Northampton	BD, NH, NV, RP, VV
Norwich	AH, CL, EX, NG, PW, VF, VG
Nottingham	AL, AU, CH, NN, NU, RA, RB, RC, RR, TO, TV, VO
Oxford	BW, FC, JO, UD, WL
Peterborough	AV, CE, EB, EG, ER, EW, FL, JE, VA, VE
Portsmouth	BK, BP, CR, DL, OR, OT, OW, PO, PX, RV, TP, TR
Preston	BV, CK, CW, EC, EO, FR, FV, HG, RN
Reading	AN, BL, CF, DP, GM, JB, JH, JM, MO, RD, RX, TF
Sheffield	AK, DT, ET, HE, HL, KU, KW, KY, WA, WB, WE, WF, WG, WJ
Shrewsbury	AW, NT, UJ, UX
Stoke-on-Trent	BF, EH, FA, RE, RF, VT
Swansea	CY, EP, TH, WN
Swindon	AM, HR, MR, MW
Taunton	YA, YB, YC, YD
Truro	AF, CV, GL, RL
Worcester	AB, NP, UY, WP

Whilst it has always been possible to retain a cherished registration this was not common until the 1990s. Prior to this most vehicles carried registrations that accurately reflected their age. When transferring a cherished registration to a vehicle the rule is that the registration number must not be younger than the vehicle. For example the registration A 4 TOM (issued 1983/4) could be put on an car built in 1990 but not one built in 1970.

Prior to the 1970s most of the vehicles in an area would carry local registrations. It was only in the 1970s as people moved about more and large organisations registered vehicles centrally that local marks ceased to be so prevalent.

The plates themselves are produced to standard sizes. Front number plates are 520 mm × 111 mm in size. Rear plates may be rectangular (520 mm × 111 mm), square (285 mm × 203 mm) or large (533 mm × 152 mm).

Since 1998 there has been an option to have a European style number plate with a blue band on the left hand side, like this:

In 2001 the system changed again to a two letter local series, two digit date identifier and three letters (AB12 CDE). The two letter local codes are different to those used for 1963 to 2001. The two digit date identifiers are as follows:

51	Sep 01 to Feb 02	05	Mar 05 to Aug 05
02	Mar 02 to Aug 02	55	Sep 05 to Feb 06
52	Sep 02 to Feb 03	06	Mar 06 to Aug 06
03	Mar 03 to Aug 03	56	Sep 06 to Feb 07
53	Sep 03 to Feb 04	07	Mar 07 to Aug 07
04	Mar 04 to Aug 04	57	Sep 07 to Feb 08
54	Sep 04 to Feb 05	and so on...	

If you want more information on this topic then two good places to start are www.dvla.gov.uk/vehicles/number_plates_registration_marks.aspx and www.en.wikipedia.org/wiki/British_car_number_plates.

A selection of cars outside the infamous Mitchell brothers' lock-up down in Walford. This is a scene on the late Tony Chlad's Walford Arches OO gauge layout using repainted die-cast toy cars.

Vehicle rallies can provide lots of useful material for modellers. This panda car would be a nice addition to a rural layout set in the early 1970s.

Road vehicles get mucky. This minibus is more brown than green on its skirt panels. Notice how the area in front of the wheels is cleaner. Most of the dirt is thrown up by the wheels.

Chapter 4: Building road vehicles

If you are interested in providing a suitable selection of road vehicles for your layout then sooner or later you will need to build a kit. This can be a worrying prospect but the good news is that not only are the skills that you need just the same as for building kits for the railway, but given that your road vehicles (probably) won't be called on to move and, if necessary, can be partially hidden by the scenery, they provide a good way to practice those skills on something that doesn't need to be perfect.

Scratchbuilding

People have been building vehicles from scratch for many years. Some are easier than others, slab sided buses or lorries are a lot easier than cars of the 1950s with all those curves. Using styrene sheet of various thicknesses you can make up the basic shape and then file the curved panels to shape. Suitable wheels and radiators can sometimes be found as spare parts or created using a bit of inventiveness.

This 4mm scale Ford Focus, scratchbuilt by James Makin, is 49mm long and about 20mm wide. It was built up from layers of plastic card filed down to give the necessary curves. James based it on measurements taken from his own car.
Photo: James Makin

John Day Ford Transit Van

This model, catalogue number TSRV03, is typical of those produced by both John Day and R Parker. It consists of just four parts: the body, the chassis, a steering wheel on a column and vacuum-formed glazing. This particular model also comes with decals so that it can be finished as either a British Rail or Wimpey owned vehicle.

The castings represent a Mk.1 short-wheelbase Transit van with a diesel engine. The diesel Transits had a different bonnet arrangement to the more usually seen petrol version and this makes a nice contrast with the models produced in the Trackside range.

After a few minutes gentle work with some wet and dry paper to fettle the castings, they were given a wash in some warm, soapy water and left to dry inside a small plastic box.

The John Day Transit kit in its entirety. Metal body, chassis and steering column, vacuum-formed glazing and decals. Kit building doesn't get much easier than this.

The completed model is more of an exercise in painting than kit assembly and makes a good starting model for the inexperienced builder.

The next day the castings were given a coat of primer from a car spray paint can. When that had dried a yellow top coat, again car spray paint, was applied to the body. The steering wheel and column assembly was fixed in place and then the chassis was brush painted dark grey.

Detail painting consisted of some black paint on the raised parts of the grille, silver bumpers, lights and door handles. Inside, the seats, steering wheel and dashboard were painted black. Dark grey tyres with silver hub caps finished the painting off.

When the paint was dry the body was given a coat of gloss varnish. When that was dry the decals were applied and left to dry. Finally a coat of matt varnish was applied to remove the 'showroom' finish.

When the varnish had dried the glazing was cut to remove the lip around the bottom. A dab of PVA adhesive was placed on the ceiling of the model and the glazing pushed into place. A couple more dabs of glue were put inside the front and rear of the body to hold the chassis in place and the model, as supplied, was complete.

You can, of course, dress the model up with registration plates, windscreen wipers, wing mirrors and a driver.

Resin Model Bus Kits

A wide variety of model bus kits have been produced in polyurethane resin. This material is well suited to limited production runs of fifty or so models. Whilst this means that a wide variety of kits have been produced by a surprising number of manufacturers, the limited production and small size of the producers means that locating and obtaining a specific model can be a difficult exercise. For those wishing to build a number of bus kits, membership of the Model Bus Federation will give access to a regular magazine, specialist shop and much useful information.

Most resin bus kits come with a single-piece body (except double-deckers which often consist of a separate upper and lower deck), chassis unit with seats cast in place, a selection of metal detail parts for radiators, steering wheels and interior partitions, a set of road wheels and the necessary glazing. Paint and decals suitable for your chosen prototype normally need to be purchased separately.

Resin is very easy to work with, it files quickly and can be cut with a razor saw or a craft knife. This means that it is easy to make small, or even large, modifications to better represent a chosen prototype. Extra parts can be made from filler or plastic sheet and fixed in place with epoxy resin or super glue.

Occasionally you will find that a resin casting is warped. This can be corrected by dunking it in hot water, which will soften the resin, and then straightening it. You will need some means of holding it in position whilst the resin cools, such as taping it to a length of wood or holding it in place with rubber bands.

As this kit produced by Paragon Models shows, most resin bus kits are fairly simple to construct, having few parts.

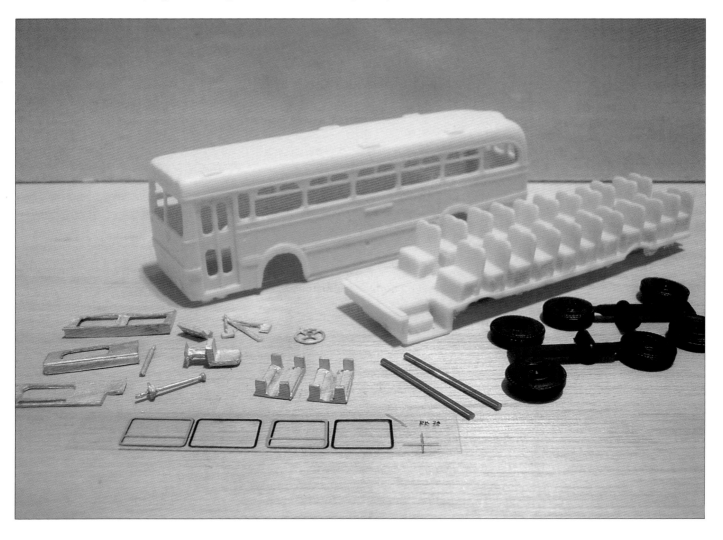

A Ribble bus of the 1950/60s built from a resin kit.

If you remove something you shouldn't have when cleaning up or modifying the parts you can use plastic and filler to repair the damage. If you actually break a resin part it can be joined using super glue and often the repair needs no further attention.

Resin parts need to be washed well in soapy water, then clean water and left to dry before being painted. Chemicals and grease on the surface of the castings will cause difficulties with paint adhering to the model if you do not do this.

As with all model road vehicles, once you have completed the basic model you can add detailing to your heart's content.

BW Models Bedford TJ Fire Appliance

BW Models produce a number of civilian emergency service vehicles as well as their large range of military vehicles. All are cast in low melting point metal and are reasonably priced. This kit is typical of the more complex road vehicle kits that are available.

The Bedford TJ was used as the basis for fire appliances built in the 1960s and early 1970s. As each fire brigade specifies its own vehicles it is difficult to produce generic models, but the TJ was a popular choice in rural areas. This particular model represents an HCB-Angus bodied Water Tender/Ladder unit purchased by Somerset Fire Brigade in 1966.

The easiest way to track down photographs for models like this is to use an internet search engine. An image search on Google turned up front and rear three-quarter views of a 1969 model purchased by Cornwall County Fire Brigade. It remained in service until the start of 1986.

The first step is to open up the box and check that you have all the parts. BW Models provide an exploded drawing and parts list which helps with the identification of some of the more mysterious pieces of metal. Comparing the parts with photos of the real thing also helps to ascertain how it all fits together.

After this you need to clean up the castings, removing any moulding lines and waste material using needle files, emery boards and wet and dry paper. Test fit the parts as you go. You will usually find that some have to be filed down in order to get a good fit.

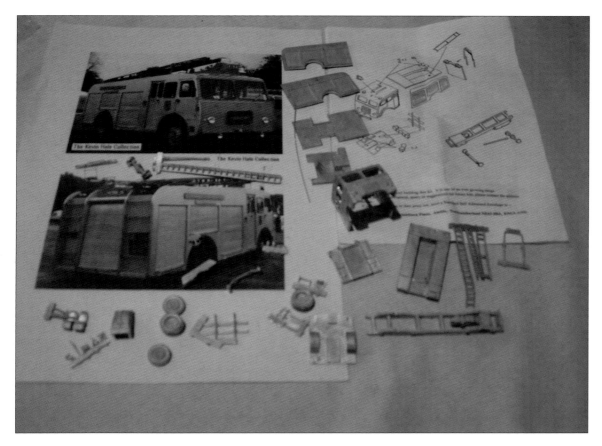

The first step is to check the kit's parts against the list, to ensure that they are all there and you know what they are. Then you can check them against the exploded diagram and photographs to see what goes where and if any modifications are necessary.

Emery boards, normally used for filing ladies' fingernails, are useful tools for removing moulding marks and excess metal from castings. The large flat area makes it easy to keep edges straight.

When using wet and dry paper to smooth a part it is best to place the wet and dry paper on the work surface, hold the part to be smoothed and use a circular motion in order to remove the material evenly. Holding the wet and dry paper or using a back and forth motion will tend to round the part's edges and corners.

Having cleaned up the cab and back panel it is time to test the fit. In this case I needed to file some of each side of the back panel to get it to sit inside the cab.

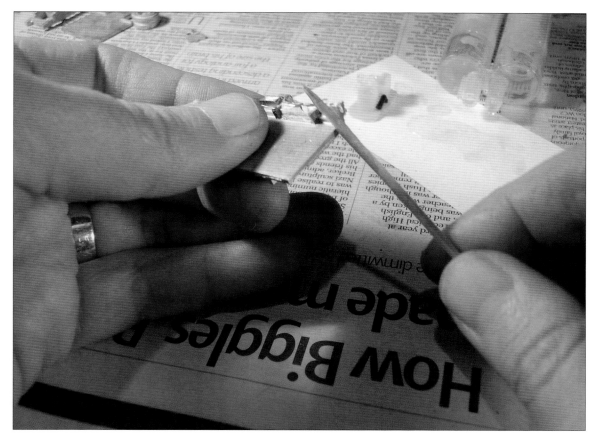

Epoxy resin not only glues parts together but also acts as a useful filler when there are small gaps between parts. One of the best tools for applying the resin is a cocktail stick – small, easy to use, cheap and disposable.

Even quick-setting epoxy resins take a few minutes to set. This means that parts need to be held together, in the correct alignment, whilst the resin hardens. Sometimes you just have to sit there and hold the pieces. Normally it is possible to use BluTack or rubber bands to hold parts together while you carry on with something else.

However careful you are, you will end up with some gaps and imperfections that need to be filled. You can use either a filler sold for modellers or ordinary car body filler. Again the humble cocktail stick is useful for applying the filler, poking it into gaps and removing the excess. A wet finger will do a good job of smoothing the filler when you have finished.

The model is made up of sub-assemblies which make it easier to paint. The body and chassis will be united after the painting has been completed.

A coat of car primer spray paint not only provides a uniform finish ready for painting but also shows up any areas where more work with files or filler is needed. Correct these blemishes now as, contrary to popular belief, a coat of paint won't hide them.

The body has now been sprayed with silver car paint and the red cab area is being brush painted using modellers' enamel paints. Note that the detail parts such as ladders haven't been fixed in place yet.

With the painting complete, decals and easily damaged detail parts have now been added ready for the final assembly. The blue lights are from a Cararama Coastguard Land Rover rather than those supplied in the kit.

The model now only needs glazing and details like number plates and wing mirrors and it will be ready to take its place on the layout.

Even a small area, such as this, can provide a lot of life and atmosphere with careful attention to road vehicles and street furniture. In the days when buses were crew-operated it was not uncommon for them to be found outside the vehicle having a chat or a cigarette whilst waiting to start their return journey.

Not all road users are wheeled. Here the local hunt is having a stirrup cup before setting out across the frozen fields. Meanwhile a bus waits in the hope of some passengers. The hunt has been a traditional sight in rural England for many years but, like snow, is becoming rarer.

CHAPTER

Chapter 5: Detailing

In this chapter I will show you how to make standard, readily available vehicles into more realistic models. The projects vary in complexity but none involve skills that cannot be mastered by any aspiring modeller. A number of tips and techniques are also covered, some of which have uses in other areas of model-making such as buildings and rolling stock. The projects are not shown in any particular order of complexity.

Austin 1100 Police Panda Car

Many of the cars from the old Minix range are readily available at swapmeets and on eBay so they make an ideal basis for detailing and conversion projects. As an example, here is how I converted the Austin 1100 into a police panda car. Searching the internet turned up a selection of photos from the West Midlands Police Museum (www.westmidlandspolicemuseum.co.uk) which included an 1100 panda car. I printed the image out as it is very annoying to go back to a site at some later point and find that the information you wanted has disappeared. The photo that I used as the basis for the model shows a West Midlands Police car in blue and white with a white roof box. The photo shows a two-door car whilst the Minix model is a four-door version. Some police forces used four-door vehicles so I chose not to modify the doors on the model.

The first job is to dismantle the model. The chassis is usually glued into the body along the inside of the bodyshell between the axles. Running a craft knife or thin screwdriver along the join will usually release the glue, allowing the chassis and glazing unit to be pulled out of the body.

The glazing and wheels will normally just lift off the chassis. Put them to one side whilst you work on the chassis unit itself.

The model has over-riders on the front and rear bumpers which are not on the vehicle in the photo. These were fitted to earlier 1100s. They can be cut off with a sharp craft knife and any surplus removed with a needle file or wet and dry paper.

As supplied the model lacks any interior so some simple seats need to be cut from plastic card. I used 60 thou card for the seat bases and 20 thou for the tops and backs. An HO scale figure was cut down to fit on the driver's seat and the driver's window was cut away from the glazing unit, using a razor saw for the vertical cuts and a craft knife for the horizontal cut. The body received a couple of coats of white paint.

The chassis has now been painted and fitted with new wheels from a Cararama Mini. The driver has also been painted and glued in place on the driving seat. His legs have been cut away so that he fits neatly into the car.

The body was brush painted overall with matt white paint, followed by light blue covering everything except the front doors. The door handles and some trim were picked out using Humbrol MetalCote aluminium paint applied with the end of a cocktail stick. This is a useful technique for touching in small details and is more controllable than a paint brush in these circumstances.

The rear lights were touched in with red and orange Humbrol Clear – these paints are designed to colour glass and so allow the silver to appear tinted.

Make Your Own Decals

When making models of road vehicles you will often find that you need lettering or a logo that is just not available as a commercial decal. Fortunately, by harnessing the computer and printer found in many homes it is possible to produce home-made decals.

The process has certain limitations. You cannot print in white or metallic colours and a light colour decal on a dark painted surface usually won't work.

The first stage is to produce the artwork using a drawing or word-processing program. You can print the design out on ordinary paper to check its size and appearance in place on the model before committing the design to production.

This is the design for the POLICE wording on the Morris 1100, which was prepared in the drawing program CorelDraw, although a word processor would have been equally effective.

POLICE   POLICE   POLICE

The design was printed onto clear decal film using a normal ink-jet printer and left to dry. You can also buy white decal film which is useful for things like registration plates and bus destination blinds. For these you print the black areas and leave the white to show through.

Always spray the varnish somewhere where there is good ventilation. In this case I took advantage of a calm day to do it in the garden.

Once the printer ink has dried the decals must be sprayed with varnish to stop the ink running when the decal is immersed in water. If the decal paper does not come with, or have a recommended fixative spray then an acrylic varnish should be used.

A tax disc was added to the windscreen using a dot of paint applied with the point of a cocktail stick. The windscreen wipers are from a Taylor Precision Models' etched set and the arms were trimmed slightly to make them a better fit. To fix them in place the windscreen was given a coat of Johnsons Klear floor polish. This dries to a tough transparent film. The wipers were simply positioned using tweezers and the occasional prod from a cocktail stick. Once the Klear dried they were firmly fixed in place.

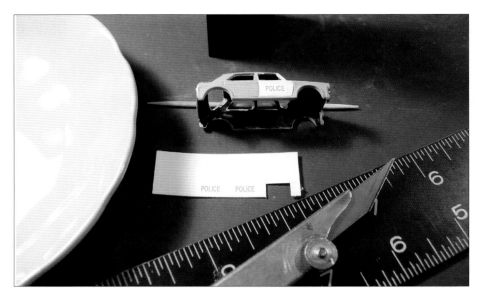

The POLICE lettering on the doors was prepared on a computer and then printed onto waterslide decal paper. The computer-produced decals are used in exactly the same way as any other waterslide decals. I prepared three so that I had a spare in case of problems. The doors were given a coat of gloss varnish in order to hide the decal film. When the varnish was dry the decals were applied to the doors and allowed to dry.

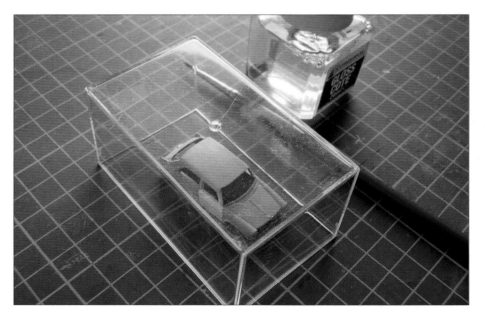

The body was given a coat of satin varnish and left to dry. A plastic lid from a Cararama model's box makes a useful cover to keep dust off the model whilst the varnish dries. Using satin varnish for the top coat avoids the high gloss finish that afflicts so many models.

With the varnish dry the car was reassembled. A police light and box was cut from the roof of a Cararama police mini by running a craft knife underneath it. This was then super glued to the 1100's roof.

Wing Mirrors

Whilst they are fiddly to make, home-made wing mirrors are a necessity when no suitable commercial item is available.

The mirrors themselves can be cut or punched from cooking foil and then attached to fuse wire arms using a small drop of super glue.

Circular mirrors, such as those on the Austin 1100 can be produced by using the shank of a suitably sized drill pressed down on to the foil placed on a cutting mat. Whilst not every mirror produced will be perfectly round, the speed of production and cost of the material allows you to discard any that you don't feel are good enough to use. The punching action tends to produce a small lip all around the mirror which will nicely represent a frame.

Apply a tiny drop of super glue to the back of the mirror and put a short length of fuse wire in place using a pair of tweezers. Leave the glue to dry and then fit the mirrors to your model.

Two small holes were drilled in the wings using a small drill in a pin chuck. A dot of super glue gel was placed underneath the holes and the wing mirror stalks were pushed through the holes into the glue. Finally the number plates were printed from the computer, cut out and glued in place with Evostick Resin W.

'I reckon it's full of stolen goods, Sarge.' A beat bobby updates his Sergeant who has declined to leave the relative comfort of the car.

Dual-door Bristol RE Bus

The ECW-bodied Bristol RE was a common sight across the country for many years and found its way into bus fleets of all sizes. The dual-door version was a town and city dweller, the improved boarding and alighting times making up for the lower seating capacity. Converting the EFE 1/76th scale die-cast model of the RE to represent a dual-door example is a project that is well within the scope of the modeller who wishes to develop their skills.

The model is held together by plastic rivets that fit onto the three metal poles that run from the roof to the chassis. Place the model in a vice, padded with foam rubber to protect it from damage, and drill two or three small holes in each of the plastic rivets. The rivets should now be loose enough that they can be pulled off with needlenose pliers.

The first step to dismantling the model is to remove the plastic rivets that hold the chassis in place.

If you retain the poles and rivets you can reassemble the model in the same way that it was originally put together. Alternatively you can break the poles off by bending them backwards and forwards, discard the rivets and glue the model back together. Removing the poles makes a big improvement to the model's appearance.

The chassis and seating unit simply slide out, after which you can remove the glazing.

You can now lift out the chassis and seating unit followed by the side glazing units and the rear window. To ease the front windscreen out you need to gently push up on the bottom pair of lugs that secure it in place from the inside until you can push them forwards. The windscreen will then slide out.

You can now mark the two cuts that you need to make on the side of the model. The new door will be fitted in place of the fourth window from the front on the nearside. Using a small square and a craft knife scribe two lines from the edge of the window down to the bottom of the side.

A razor saw is the best tool for cutting through the model's tough metal.

Cut out the opening for the new door using a razor saw. Cut carefully along the marked lines. The metal is tough so let the saw do the work and don't try to rush.

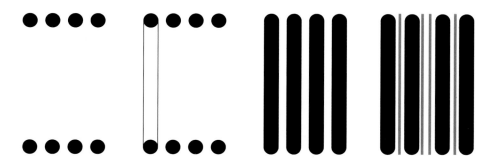

Cutting the door from plastic sheet. Left to right: drill eight holes for the top and bottom of the windows; join the holes by cutting with a craft knife; remove the waste and trim any rough edges with a file; scribe the door leaves with a craft knife.

The door is cut from styrene sheet, sized to match the front door. The four long windows can be formed by drilling two lines of holes and then cutting between them. The individual leaves of the door can be marked by scribing between them with the craft knife.

A large flat file will help to clean up the cut edges and give a straight sided opening for the new door.

If you intend to repaint the model then you will need to strip the old paint off before you fix the new door in place. The door can be glued in position using epoxy resin and then you can paint the model.

Once the paint is dry the new door can be glazed by gluing a piece of clear plastic sheet behind it. The nearside glazing strip needs to have the centre window, corresponding to the new door's position, cut out. As a minimum you will need to remove the two pairs of seats alongside the new doorway from the seating unit. These can easily be cut away with a craft knife. You may wish to add more details to the interior whilst you are at it.

A section of the edge of the chassis needs to be cut away to clear the new door. The chassis is made of plastic and can be cut using a craft knife. Trim down the section that was cut away and stick it in place underneath the door.

If you have repainted the whole bus you will need to buy some decals to reinstate the printed radiator grille. These are available from Bus Fare.

The complete model, finished in NBC Potteries livery.

Ford Transit

The Cararama Ford Transit is supplied in a number of plain colours. The white version is ideal not only for representing the ubiquitous 'white van' but also as a basis for vehicles as diverse as speed camera vans, ambulances and delivery vans. This exercise is a little less ambitious and simply involves adding sign-writing to an otherwise unaltered van.

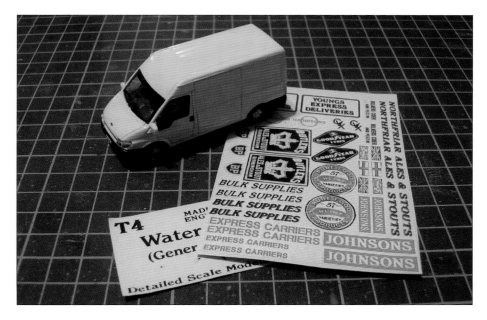

All this project takes is a Cararama Transit, a sheet of decals and a little of your time.

I chose the yellow-painted version to make a nice background to the red decals that I intended to use. The decals came from the Langley Miniature Models' range and whilst the decal sheets are listed as being to 1/76th scale many of the items on them seemed too large for use on vehicles.

Test the fit of the decals before you get them wet. Once they are off the backing sheet it is too late to change your mind.

The decals are cut from the main sheet using a craft knife and steel ruler then checked for size against the model. It is far better to establish if there are any problems now, before the decal has been soaked and is ready to apply.

These decals had been stored for a while and had a tendency to break up into pieces when soaked in water. To solve this I gave the whole sheet a coat of gloss varnish and left it to dry. The decals can still be soaked off the backing paper, but the varnish helps to keep them intact.

Soak the decal in water for about ten seconds and then put it in position, still on its backing paper. Wait until the decal releases from the backing paper, adding an extra drop of water if necessary, then hold one corner in place with a cocktail stick whilst you slide the backing paper out from underneath. I find that the pointed blade of a craft knife is a good tool for this as it can dig into the backing paper.

Smooth the decal down with a paint brush that has been dipped in a decal setting solution such as Humbrol Decalfix. This will soften the decal and help it to sit over any raised detail on the model. Gently dab any excess water or decal setting solution away with a paper tissue and leave the model to dry. Only do one side at a time, trying to hurry and fix all the decals in one sitting will often lead to you pushing one or more out of place whilst you are working on the other side of the model.

Just adding decals has given this van an identity. There is plenty of scope to add more details, including converting it from left to right hand drive.

Finally, if your model will be a static scenic item then you may be able to get away with just applying decals to the sides that will be seen on your layout. If, for example, this van was to be parked in the corner of a walled yard, there would be no point in doing the rear and nearside as they would never be seen – leaving some spare decals for another vehicle, or possibly signs on a building.

Ford Zephyr Estate

Battered old toy cars can be found at car boot sales, swapmeets and on eBay. Some are suitable candidates for conversion into models suitable for use on a model railway.

The starting point for this project was a battered, repainted toy purchased on eBay.

This project started as a rather battered, repainted Husky Ford Zephyr 6 Estate. The first task was to take it to pieces. This was achieved by drilling out the three rivets that hold the body and chassis together.

The three rivets visible underneath the model hold the body and chassis together. These need to be drilled out so that the model can be taken to bits.

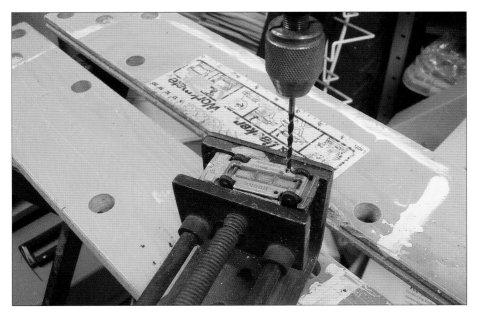

Place the model upside down in a vice and, using a drill that is a slightly larger diameter than the rivet heads, drill down until the chassis comes free.

You can now remove the chassis and interior.

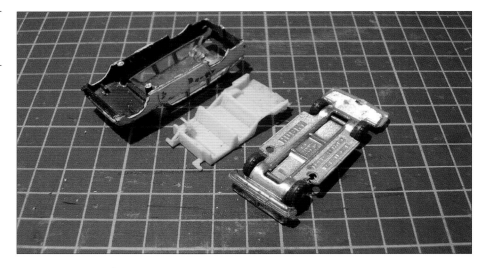

There is another rivet in the body that needs to be drilled out carefully so that you can remove the glazing unit and rear tailgate. If you drill too far you will go through the roof, so proceed carefully and slowly. I always use a hand drill for rivets, it would be easy to go too far with an electric drill.

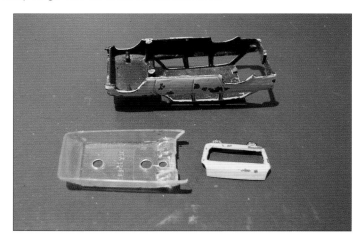

The tailgate and glazing separated from the body.

The body and tailgate should then be placed in some paint stripper to remove the original paintwork. I used Nitromors, available from places like Halfords. Be very careful when using products like this and take heed of the warnings on the container. Stubborn paint can be removed by scrubbing under running water with an old toothbrush.
A foil food container makes a useful paint stripper bath, either recycled from a take-away meal or purchased specially for the purpose.

Once the paint has been stripped and the model given a wash to remove any remaining trace of paint stripper it is time to start rebuilding it.

The painted body, chassis and seating unit along with some new wheels from a Cararama model.

Once you have a pristine bodyshell you can turn your attention to the chassis. I decided to replace the Matchbox wheels with a set from a Cararama Austin Healey. The Cararama range can often be found at reasonable prices in pound shops and similar establishments. At that price they are worth buying as a source of wheels even if you don't need the rest of the model. Good wheels go a long way to making a convincing model.

The body was then sprayed with car primer paint and, when that had dried, sprayed with car body paint from an aerosol can. Again, follow the instructions on the can and you will be amazed at how good a paint finish you can obtain.

The chrome trim was painted with Humbrol MetalCote aluminium coloured paint and the rear light clusters painted with Humbrol Clear (a sort of tinted varnish) in red and orange. Alternatively you can use a thin wash of standard paint. Don't make the brake lights and indicators too bright, they just don't look like that in reality. The interior had a coat of yellowish paint with the steering wheel painted black.

The basic model rebuilt with its new paint job. Whilst it is nice as it is, adding some details will improve its appearance greatly.

Drilling holes for the wing mirrors requires a small drill. When actually doing the drilling it is best to place a small piece of masking tape on the body to stop the drill slipping and scratching the paint when you start to turn it.

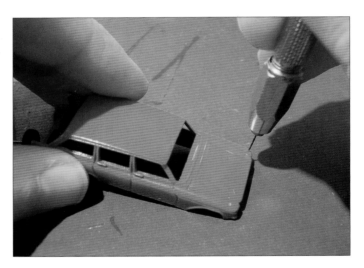

Using a pin chuck I drilled two small holes on the front wings to mount etched wing mirrors. I used a strip of masking tape to protect the paintwork and stop the drill from slipping. The wing mirrors came from Taylor Precision Models and come on a fret with three sets of wing mirrors, three sets of windscreen wipers, three steering wheels and even three rear view mirrors. The wing mirrors were superglued in place; you'll need tweezers to hold them whilst you position them as they are very fiddly.

The etched wing mirrors are small and fiddly. You will need tweezers and patience to mount them in their holes.

The glazing unit was put back in the body, held in place with a small drop of PVA adhesive. When the adhesive had set I turned my attention to the front windscreen which had some scratches on it. A coat of Johnson's Klear floor polish (honestly) works wonders to restore the glazing. It also does a good job of holding etched windscreen wipers in place (position them with a cocktail stick). Wash your brush out in water when you have finished and leave the windscreen to dry. As a final touch dab the end of a cocktail stick into some paint and use it to print a tax disc on the inside of the windscreen. A small piece of clear plastic, from some waste packaging, was cut and glued inside the tailgate to act as the rear window.

Now you can reunite the interior and chassis with the body. The tailgate was fixed open using epoxy resin. This will allow the vehicle to be posed in a scene with someone loading it and saves work trying to disguise the join between the parts. A small touch of epoxy resin at the rear of the chassis will keep things together. All that is left is to add some number plates.

The finished estate is ready for loading by the railway arches.

Mini Traveller

The Mini Traveller with its characteristic wooden framing was an interesting style. Cararama produce it in their range of near 1/76th scale models. Unfortunately the wood framing is cast in place so it isn't possible to convert the model to a standard estate just by removing some paint. If you want such a model you will need to cut windows into a van version.

Here is a model straight out of the box (left) compared with one that has had the printed windscreen wipers removed (right).

The first step is to remove the printed windscreen wipers so that they can be replaced with etched metal ones. To protect the chrome windscreen surround I used strips of masking tape. The printed wipers were removed by rubbing gently with a cotton bud that had been dipped in nail varnish remover.

Removing Printed Detail

When detailing and modifying model road vehicles you will often find that you need to remove printed detail from a model. This can be windscreen wipers printed on glazing, fleet names on buses or other features that you need to replace. These features are added to the model on top of the normal paintwork by a process known as tampo printing. A special rubber pad is used to print the details onto the surface of the model. The trick is to remove the detail printing without damaging the paintwork below. Two methods are commonly used.

The first is to use a cotton bud dipped in a car paint restorer, such as T-Cut, and gently rub away the printing. By working carefully and gently it is normally possible to completely remove the printed detail without damaging the paint underneath. The paint restorer is a mild abrasive that rubs away the top layer of paint, in this case the printing. This does tend to leave a gloss finish on the revealed paintwork but that can easily be fixed with a coat of varnish.

The second method is to use nail varnish remover in the same way. This has a chemical action rather than an abrasive one and can soften the paint underneath. Most nail varnish removers are now coloured and this can leave a tint on light coloured paint if you are heavy handed.

Whichever liquid you use it is important to mask the area around the printing that you want removed so that you do not accidentally rub away something that you wish to keep. Masking tape is ideal for this purpose and should be removed as soon as you have finished work. Once the printed detail has been removed a quick rinse will remove any remaining fluid.

One last suggestion: sometimes it is possible to remove the detail printing by gently rubbing it with the edge of your fingernail. It only works occasionally, but always try it first, just in case.

Next I turned my attention to adding a little rust around the wheel arches and at the bottom of the doors. Cars made in the 1960s and 70s often suffered from severe rusting problems. A little work with a fine paint brush and some suitable coloured paint will give the impression of a vehicle past its prime. Whilst the paint was out I added a tax disc to the windscreen by applying a dot of paint with the end of a cocktail stick.

Etched windscreen wipers were fitted to the windscreen and wing mirrors to holes drilled in the front wings; both came from a TPM etch. The windscreen wipers were fixed in place with a drop of Johnsons Klear whilst the wing mirrors were secured with super glue gel. Tweezers are essential when handling such small parts. You will also find that a couple of cocktail sticks are really useful for pushing the windscreen wipers into position.

The finished article. Whilst it looks careworn it is still good for a few miles yet.

The final stage was to add number plates. These can be generated on a computer, printed onto paper and stuck in place, or you can purchase commercial decals. The front number plate is mounted below the front bumper so you either need to put the decal on a small bit of plastic or leave it on its backing paper and just glue it in place.

In the 1950s and 1960s it could be quite common to find buses outnumbering other road vehicles in some urban areas. Here a trio of municipal vehicles converge on a suburban street whilst the postman makes a collection in his Morris van.

A fair number of double-deckers were built to what was called 'lowbridge' design so that they could fit under low bridges. The taller design was, unsurprisingly, called 'highbridge'. Here a lowbridge Bristol L squeezes under a girder bridge on a diorama built by the late Eric Newlove. To gain extra headroom when going under arched bridges tall vehicles often use the centre of the road, causing traffic coming in the opposite direction to stop.

The Second World War brought many problems to vehicle users. The lack of fuel reduced the number of vehicles on the road and those that did needed to abide by special regulations. Headlights were masked, mudguards needed white markings to aid visibility and on many buses the windows were covered with blast netting. This scene depicts an area of London during the Blitz.

Schools have always provided bus operators with a large amount of traffic. The school run with parents vying for parking spaces outside the gates is a relatively recent phenomenon. For many years pupils would walk, cycle or catch the bus.

Chapter 6: Making them move

The late Tony Chlad's Walford Arches layout brought moving road vehicles to the attention of many exhibition goers. The trains on the viaduct at the rear of the layout acted as a backdrop to the roadway and trolley bus terminus in front. This is a posed scene; not all of the vehicles shown are motorised – and if they were, trying to control them would be an interesting exercise.

A view of the late Tony Chlad's 'Walford Arches' layout which featured operating trolleybuses and other road vehicles.

Part of the fascination of model railways is that they move, or at least the trains do. Even a crude model rushing around an oval of track can capture some of the spirit of the real thing. Unfortunately our moving trains all too often journey through landscapes where the rest of the world appears to have been immobilised by some supernatural force. Flags, people, animals, road vehicles – all are stationary as our model train flashes past.

With careful selection and placement of figures and vehicles the static nature of things outside the railway fence can be minimised. Road vehicles can be parked, people can be chatting in groups, cows lying in a field. But an even better solution is to provide moving road traffic to provide a believable backdrop.

In reality road traffic is complex and constantly changing but fortunately in model form you can give the impression of people going about their business with a small number of vehicles. The viewers' minds will fill in the rest, just as they accept the limitations of the railway scene as modelled.

With two or three vehicles moving around your layout, disappearing behind buildings and reappearing elsewhere, negotiating junctions and passing parked vehicles, the illusion of a living town served by your model railway will be greatly enhanced.

The trick is to make the vehicles move without any obvious means of guidance which would ruin the illusion of reality. This excludes slot-car type systems which provide power and guidance but require an obvious trench along the road. Remote control is possible but would require continuous individual control of each vehicle, although it would offer the ultimate in flexibility. Fortunately it is possible to combine magnetic guidance with on-board battery power to provide operating vehicles that can be routed and stopped remotely.

The German firm of Faller are the market leaders in this field and provide motorised vehicles that follow a hidden guide wire in HO, TT and even N scale. Whilst the range in the smaller two scales is very limited, the HO range includes a wide range of European vehicles, including articulated and rigid trucks, vans, buses and cars.

The Faller CarSystem consists of:

- A steel guide wire buried under the road surface.
- A magnetic guide arm linked to a steering front axle.
- A rechargeable battery to provide power.
- An electric motor driving the rear axle.
- A magnetically operated switch to start and stop the motor.
- Magnets under the road to stop the vehicle.

This allows virtually invisible guidance and control, albeit in a basic manner, of model road vehicles. As supplied the vehicles cannot reverse and there is no speed control but neither of these problems affects their use as a living backdrop to a model railway. It is possible to fit Faller mechanisms into UK outline vehicles for use with 4mm scale British outline layouts. Having got some moving road vehicles it is easy to get carried away with enthusiasm. Remember there are limits to how much one person can control at once – especially if they are trying to operate a model railway too.

Dimensions	Actual	1/76th scale	Notes
Minimum radius	15cm	11.5m (37' 9")	This will vary with wheelbase and steering lock.
Recommended minimum radius	18.5cm	14m (45' 11")	This will allow most vehicles to operate smoothly.
Recommended distance between guide wires (opposite direction)	6cm	4.6m (15' 1")	This measurement allows for a constant distance for both curved and straight roads. On straight roads this can be reduced to 4.5cm.
Minimum distance between guide wires (same direction)	4mm	0.3m (1')	This is for two guide wires on the same carriageway. Obviously the vehicles following each wire cannot pass each other.
Maximum operational gradient	7% (1 in 14)		As batteries discharge the gradient climbing ability (and speed) of the vehicle gets less.

There are two main drawbacks to the system as supplied. Firstly, the models are to HO (1/87th) scale of mainland European prototypes; secondly, they are, for a scenic adjunct, quite expensive.

Fortunately one of the 'Start Sets' comes with an ideal vehicle for British model railways: a Series I Ford Transit van. This is suitable for any layout based from around 1965 to 1990 or thereabouts. As the model has opaque glazing and no interior detail it doesn't even have the steering wheel on the wrong side. With the various sizes of Ford Transit that were produced it is easy for the observer to accept it as a small Transit rather than an under scale (for 'OO') model. The 'Start Sets' come with basic models that lack some of the finer details and mechanical sophistication of the vehicles in the main range, but this does mean that they are cheaper despite coming with a battery charger, coil of guide wire and sundry accessories. In the case of the Ford Transit model the rechargeable battery gives

The contents of the Faller 161513 'Start Set' includes all the parts needed to get started with motorised road vehicles.

about 30 minutes of continuous operation from a 7 hour charge. At the time of writing the Ford Transit 'Start Set' (catalogue number 161513) is available from UK model shops for around £50.

Constructing the Roadway

There are a number of techniques for constructing the roadway but the key factors are:

- It must be smooth. Any bumps, lumps or hollows can cause the steering arm to loose contact with the guide wire, resulting in the vehicle veering off course out of control.
- The guide wire must be just below the road surface. Again, if the wire dips too far below the surface the steering arm can lose contact with it.

The guide wire can be installed on any flat surface, even an existing road on your layout provided it is, or can be made, sufficiently smooth.

1. First you need to mark the course of the wire, allowing sufficient clearance for oncoming vehicles, kerbs and so on.

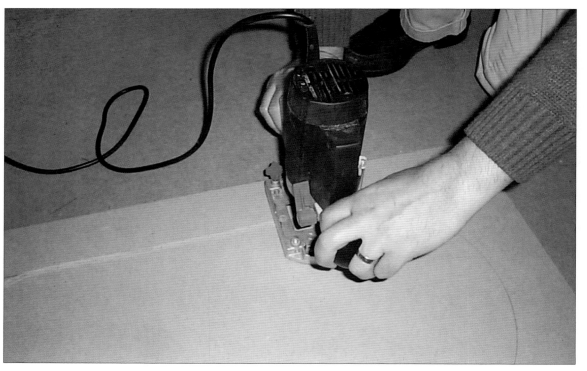

2. Use a router to cut a channel for the guide wire. The channel should be slightly deeper than the thickness of the wire. Typically the smallest router bit to create a flat bottomed channel will give a 4mm wide channel. Try to keep the channel centred along the route that you have marked.

   Once you have cut the groove smooth down any rough spots and then clean all the dust out of it using a brush or vacuum cleaner.

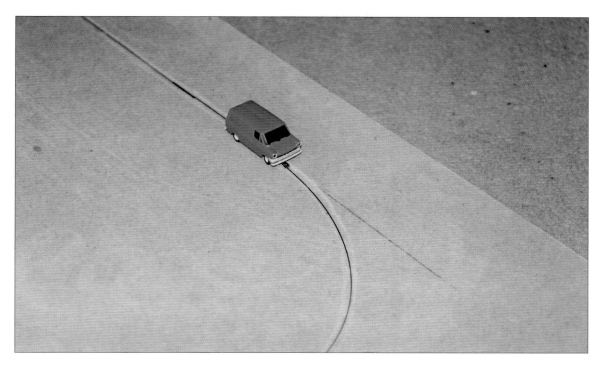

3. Cut narrow strips of double-sided tape and place them along the groove. Stick the guide wire in place on top of it. Once the circuit is complete you can give your vehicle a test drive and check the clearances.

4. Where the guide wire has to cross over, one of the wires needs to be cut to fit. For the test run place a length of Scotch Magic Tape over the crossing so that the guide arm and road wheels can get over the crossing.

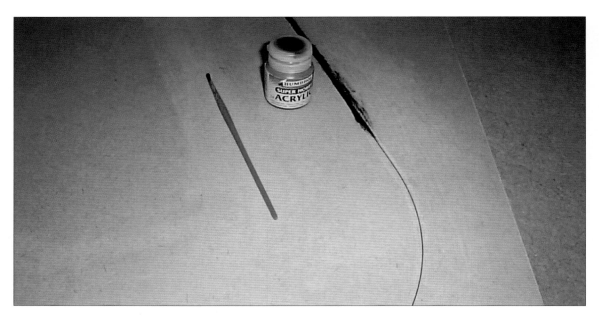

5. When all the wire has been fixed firmly in place both wire and tape get a coat of paint to seal the steel wire against rust.

6. Mix up some of the plaster supplied with the vehicle and fill the groove. It should be smoothed level with the road.
    Once the first coat is dry fill any depressions with more plaster. Sand down any areas that are proud of the wire. Repeat until you have a road surface that is level and has the wire flush with its surface. Keep testing with the vehicle until you get faultless operation.
    Use the acrylic paint supplied with the set to paint the road and then add road markings.

Once you have got a taste for motorised road vehicles you can add features such as magnets to stop vehicles and working junctions. Faller vehicles can be used to power British outline vehicles, Faller steering axles can be used with home-built chassis or you can even build your own steering axles.
    Here is an example showing how to motorise a UK outline model, in this case an EFE die-cast BET single deck bus. The BET bus has a wheelbase that is almost the same as one of the Faller models that has been available in starter sets for a number of years, the Mercedes Benz O.405 bus.

Before you do anything to modify a Faller model you should always check that it works properly. It is far too late to send it back once you have started to modify it.

The first step is to test that the bus works correctly, as once you start to modify it the guarantee will be invalidated. If you don't yet have a roadway on which to run it tape a circuit of guide wire down on a board.

Whilst the surgery needed to fit the Mercedes O.405 chassis into an EFE BET bus looks extensive, it is a simple matter of cutting along panel lines on the plastic body.

The roof and glazing unclips leaving you with a chassis that looks like the bus at the rear of the photo. Taking a deep breath you need to cut away the plastic along the side body mouldings and at the front until your chassis ends up looking like the one at the front.

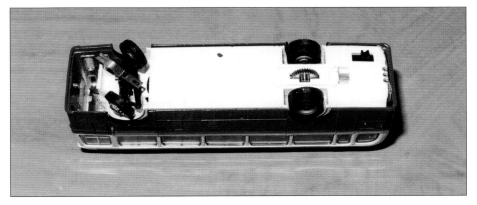

The Faller chassis is a neat fit in the EFE body. Note that the rear of the chassis has to be cut away almost to the charging socket. A small piece of insulating tape inside the rear of the body will protect against accidental short circuits from the metal body.

This motorised chassis was built using a Faller front axle, plastic sheet, readily available motor and gears and a few other parts. This is a far more economical way to create working vehicles than adapting Faller models. The power is supplied by a pair of AA batteries mounted between the front and rear wheel arches.

The EFE model needs to be dismantled and the chassis discarded. Glue the windows in and then test fit the Faller chassis. You should find that it is a snug fit. With a bit of trimming you can also refit the EFE interior. The resulting model is then ready to roll.

Sometimes a bit of ingenuity is needed to motorise a model. The cab unit of this articulated lorry doesn't appear to offer much scope to hide a motor but, as the second photo shows, a bit of lateral thinking can work wonders. Whilst the motor is mounted on the cab unit the battery is in the trailer. Brass strips act as rubbing contacts to transfer the electrical power from the trailer to the motor.

This Scammell shows that even three-wheelers are potential candidates for motorisation.
The Faller range even includes a motor scooter, albeit an unpowered one that is towed along
behind a car. This does suggest a scheme for a line of traffic. The first vehicle could be
powered and tow two or three vehicles that are just fitted with steering axles.
If anyone tries it, please let me know how you get on.

Another way to provide moving traffic as a backdrop to a layout is to fix vehicles to a moving belt that runs along the back of the layout, disappearing off scene on either side behind large buildings. The vehicles appear to pass in a continuous stream, returning underneath the layout to reappear again and again.

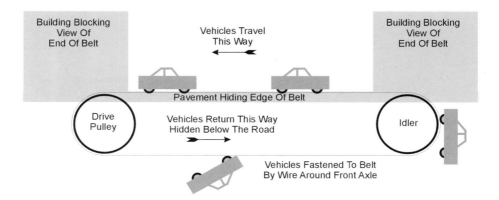

Lorries were loaded and unloaded in goods yards and factories up and down the country. This view shows a BRS flatbed being loaded with car parts. Note the tarpaulin sheeting ready for use and the two men waiting to guide the crate into position. This scene would make an interesting cameo on a 1950s or 1960s period model.
Photo: Author's collection

Appendix A: UK Manufacturers and Suppliers

Please note that unless otherwise indicated all the suppliers below deal by mail order only and do not accept personal callers. In most cases there is a charge for their price lists.

A's Models of Bolton
Die-cast model and kit retailer
Mail order only
PO Box 514
Bolton
BL1 5YD
Tel: 01204 467961
www.asmodelsofbolton.co.uk

ABS Models
4mm scale vehicle kits
Mail order only
36 Field Barn Drive
Weymouth
DT4 0ED
www.keykits.net

Bustrans
4mm scale decals and paints for buses
Mail order only
Havyngton Lodge
Churchthorpe
Fulstow
Louth
LN11 0XL
Tel: 01507 363639

B.W. Models
4mm scale white metal kits
Mail order only
Hillcrest
Kirk Brae
Cuminestown
Turriff
AB53 5YZ

Faller CarSystem
Motorised vehicles, (see Chapter 6)
UK distributor
Gaugemaster Controls plc
Gaugemaster House
Ford Road
Arundel
BN18 0BN
Tel: 01903 884488
Fax: 01903 884377
www.gaugemaster.com

John Day
4mm scale car, van and lorry kits
Mail order only
8 St Aidan's Road
East Dulwich
London
SE22 0RP

Fanfare Transport moulds
Bus kits built to order
Mail order only
c/o 2 Haig Road West
Plaistow
London
E13 9LH

Fox Transfers
4mm scale road vehicle decals and paints
Mail order only
138 Main Street
Markfield
LE67 9UX
Tel: 01530 242801
www.fox-transfers.co.uk

Harburn Hamlet
4mm scale vehicle loads and street furniture
67 Elm Row
Edinburgh
EH7 4AQ
Tel: 0131 556 3233
www.harburnhobbies.co.uk

Lancer Models
4mm scale bus kits, Midland Red vehicles
Mail order only
56 Cymberline Way
Rugby
CV22 6LA

Langley Models
White metal vehicle kits and scenic accessories in a variety of scales
166 Three Bridges Road
Crawley
RH10 1LE
Tel: 0870 0660 416
www.langleymodels.co.uk

LGM Scale Models And Kits
4mm scale pre-war vehicle kits
Mail order only
55 Edge View Walk
Kinver
Stourbridge
DY7 6AY
Tel: 01384 878504
www.lgmscalemodelsandkits.co.uk

Little Bus Company
4mm scale resin bus kits
Mail order only
LBC Models Ltd
6 Appleyard
Haworth Close
Halifax
Tel: 01422 301600
www.little-bus.com

Mabex Products
Road vehicle decals
Mail order only
PO Box 52
Tunbridge Wells
TN4 9ZS

Modelmaster
Road vehicle decals
31 Crown Street
Ayr
KA8 8AG
Tel: 01292 289770
www.modelmasterdecals.com

Paragon Kits
4mm scale bus kits and parts
Mail order only
206 St James Park Road
Northampton
NN5 5EU

R Parker
4mm scale car and van kits
Mail order only
19 Oaklands
Malvern Wells
WR14 4JE

Phoenix Precision Paints
Road vehicle paints
PO Box 8238
Chelmsford
CM1 7WY
Tel: 01268 730549
www.phoenix-paints.co.uk

Pirate Models
4mm scale bus kits
7 Horsham Lane
Upchurch
Sittingbourne
ME9 7AL
Tel: 01634 233144

P.S.G. Models
4mm scale bus and lorry kits
Mail order only
5 Birch Meadow
Broseley
TF12 5LL
Tel: 01952 883751

Road Transport Images
Kits and conversion parts for 4mm
scale lorries
Mail order only
17 Foxdene Road
Seasalter
Whitstable
CT5 4QY

Doug Roseaman Engineering
4mm scale fairground and lorry kits
101 Westbrook
Bromham
Chippenham
SN15 2EE

Roxley Models
Kit and ready-built post office
vehicles
Mainly 1/48th scale
4 Beckley Parade
Great Bookham
Surrey
Tel: 01372 452976
www.roxleymodels.co.uk

RTC Models
4mm scale bus kits, parts and decals
Mail order only
24 Rosslyn Crescent
Harrow
HA1 2RZ
Tel: 020 8861 0900

Terry Russell Trams
7mm scale tram kits and parts
Mail order only
'Chaceside'
St Leonards Park
Horsham
RH13 6EG
www.terryrusselltrams.co.uk

Scale Link Ltd
4mm scale vehicle kits
Visitors by appointment
19 Applins Farm Business Centre
Farrington
DT11 8RA
Tel: 01747 811817
www.scalelink.co.uk

Scalescenes
On-line ordering only
2 and 4mm scale road surface,
pavements and signs
www.scalescenes.com

Roger Smith
Self-adhesive road markings, printed
card road signs
Mail order only
121 Wellsford Avenue
Wells Green
Solihull
West Midlands
B92 8HB
Tel: 0121 743 4674

Springside Models
4mm scale vehicle kits
2 Springside Cottages
Dornafield Road
Ipplepen
Newton Abbot
TQ12 5SJ
Tel: 01803 813749
www.springsidemodels.com

Taylor Precision Models
4mm scale vehicle kits and parts
Mail order only
Unit 235
Stratford Workshop
Burford Road
London
E15 2SP
www.tpmodels.co.uk

Ten Commandments
4mm scale detailing parts and lorry
loads
100C High Street
Cowdenbeath
KY4 9NF
Tel: 01383 610820
www.cast-in-stone.co.uk

Appendix B: Periodicals, Clubs and Societies

The Model Bus Federation
Society for bus modellers. Offers a
monthly journal, local area meetings,
mail order shop for kits and parts.
MBF Publicity Officer
Lower Bank House
High Street
Caverswall
Stoke-on-Trent
ST11 9EF
www.model-bus-fed.org.uk

Model Buses
Quarterly magazine devoted to bus
modelling.
Model Buses
21 Forde Avenue
Bromley
BR1 3EU

**National Association of Road
Transport Modellers**
Society for road transport modellers.
Offers a bi-monthly newsletter.
NARTM
49 Holgate Road
York
YO2 4AA
Email: graham49@talktalk.net

Appendix C: Selective 4mm Scale Model Listing

Most of the models in this listing are shown in the accompanying timeline. The timeline allows you to pick matching vehicles for a given year. The green blocks show when each vehicle was in production and the red blocks show when it would still be likely to be seen on the road. Whilst you can, of course, still use a vehicle after the end of the orange block, bear in mind that it would be old and uncommon rather than an everyday sight.

BW Models
White metal kits with interior.
Land Rover Discovery
Bedford TJ Fire Appliance
Volvo FL6 Fulton Wylie Fire Appliance
Volvo FL6/Dennis Fire Appliance

Canterbury Miniature Commercials (CMC)
White metal kits with interior.
Austin A40 Devon
Austin FX3 Taxi
Standard Vanguard I

Cararama
Die-cast metal with interior.
These vehicles vary in scale. The table below shows the approximate scale of a selection of models.

BMW 3 series	1/72
BMW Isetta (Bubble car)	1/75
BMW X5	1/72
Ford Capri Mk.1	1/71
Ford Transit Mk.3	1/72
Land Rover 109	1/72
Land Rover Range Rover	1/72
Lexus GS300	1/73
Mazda MX5 (1998 style)	1/73
Mercedes Sprinter Van	1/70
Mercedes Benz C class	1/76
MGB	1/72
Mini Cooper (Original style)	1/71
Mini Cooper (New style)	1/70
Morgan Plus Eight	1/72
Peugeot 206	1/73
Renault Trafic	1/72
VW Beetle (Old style)	1/71
VW Beetle (New style)	1/72
VW Passat estate	1/65
VW Transporter	1/73
Willy's Jeep	1/72

Corgi/Lledo Trackside
Die-cast metal.
Austin VA (Noddy) van
Bedford CA Mk.II van
Bedford HA van
ERF LV lorries
Foden S21 lorries
Ford Anglia van
Ford Transit van
Morris J2 van
Morris LD van
Scammell Scarab
Scammell Townsman

Husky
Die-cast metal with interior.
The following models are suitable for use with 4mm scale models:
Citroen DS Safari   (1959–67)
Ford Zephyr Mk.3 Estate   (1962–66)
Lancia Flaminia   (1957–70)
Mercedes 220   (1959–65)

John Day
White metal kits with interior.
Austin 8
Austin A70 Hereford
Ford Consul Mk.I
Standard Eight
Standard Vanguard III

EFE
Die-cast metal with interior.
Austin-Healey Sprite
Bedford TK lorries
Bristol VR bus
Leyland National bus
Leyland Olympian bus
MGB Roadster
Triumph Vitesse Mk.2 Convertible

Langley
White metal kits with interior.
Austin FX4 Taxi

Lima
Plastic. No interior.
Ford Capri

Matchbox/Lesney
Die-cast metal. No interior.
These vehicles vary in scale. The table below shows the approximate scale of a selection of models. Some of these are unglazed.

Citroen DS	1/76
Ford Corsair	1/71
Ford Zodiac Mk.2	1/71
Ford Zephyr Mk.3	1/71
Jaguar Mk.2	1/72
Jaguar Mk.10	1/72
Jaguar XK140	1/76
Mercedes 220SE	1/73
Morris 1000	1/72
Rolls Royce Phantom	1/74
Vauxhall FA Victor	1/72
Vauxhall FB Victor Estate	1/71
Vauxhall PA Cresta	1/74

Minix
Plastic. Some with interior.
Austin 1800 Mk.I
Austin A60
Ford Anglia Mk.3
Ford Corsair
Hillman Imp Mk.I
Hillman Minx Series V/VI
Morris 1100 Mk.I
Simca 1300
Sunbeam Alpine Series IV/V
Triumph 2000 Mk.I
Vauxhall Cresta Estate
Vauxhall Victor 101
Vauxhall Viva HA

R Parker
White metal kits with interior.
Ford Anglia 105E Mk.3
Ford Zodiac Mk.2
Morris J4 10/12cwt van

Springside
White metal kits with interior.
Austin A35
Land Rover Series 3 swb
Mini Clubman
Mini Countryman
Mini Mk.I/II
Morris Minor 1000
Range Rover
Rover 2200
Triumph 2500 (Saloon and Estate)
Triumph Herald (Saloon, Convertible and Estate)

TPM
Resin kits with interior.
Austin Maxi (projected model)
Ford Capri Ghia
Ford Escort L 3-door
Vauxhall Viva (2-door and estate)

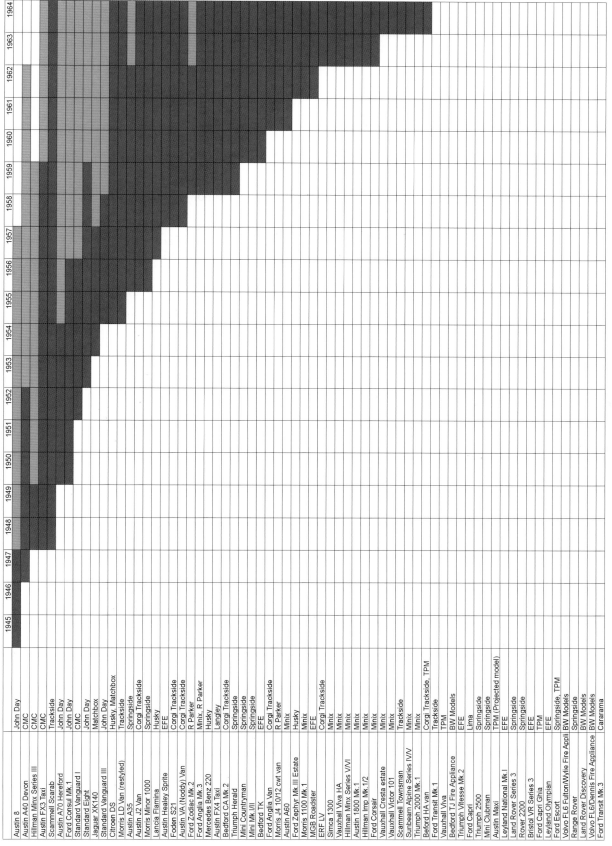

		1945	1946	1947	1948	1949	1950	1951	1952	1953	1954	1955	1956	1957	1958	1959	1960	1961	1962	1963	1964
Austin 8	John Day																				
Austin A40 Devon	CMC																				
Hillman Minx Series III	CMC																				
Austin FX3 Taxi	CMC																				
Scammell Scarab	Trackside																				
Austin A70 Hereford	John Day																				
Ford Consul Mk.1	John Day																				
Standard Vanguard I	CMC																				
Standard Eight	John Day																				
Jaguar XK140	Matchbox																				
Standard Vanguard III	John Day																				
Citroen DS	Husky, Matchbox																				
Morris LD Van (restyled)	Trackside																				
Austin A35	Springside																				
Austin J2 Van	Corgi Trackside																				
Morris Minor 1000	Springside																				
Lancia Flamina	Husky																				
Austin Healey Sprite	EFE																				
Foden S21	Corgi Trackside																				
Austin VA (Noddy) Van	Corgi Trackside																				
Ford Zodiac Mk.2	R Parker																				
Ford Anglia Mk.3	Minix, R Parker																				
Mercedes Benz 220	Husky																				
Austin FX4 Taxi	Langley																				
Bedford CA Mk.2	Corgi Trackside																				
Triumph Herald	Springside																				
Mini Countryman	Springside																				
Mini Mk.I/II	Springside																				
Bedford TK	EFE																				
Ford Anglia Van	Corgi Trackside																				
Morris J4 10/12 cwt van	R Parker																				
Austin A60	Minix																				
Ford Zephyr Mk.III Estate	Husky																				
Morris 1100 Mk.1	Minix																				
MGB Roadster	EFE																				
ERF LV	Corgi Trackside																				
Simca 1300	Minix																				
Vauxhall Viva HA	Minix																				
Hillman Minx Series V/VI	Minix																				
Austin 1800 Mk.1	Minix																				
Hillman Imp Mk.1/2	Minix																				
Ford Corsair	Minix																				
Vauxhall Cresta estate	Minix																				
Vauxhall Victor 101	Minix																				
Scammell Townsman	Trackside																				
Sunbeam Alpine Series IV/V	Minix																				
Triumph 2000 Mk.1	Minix																				
Beford HA van	Corgi Trackside, TPM																				
Ford Transit Mk.1	Trackside																				
Vauxhall Viva	TPM																				
Bedford TJ Fire Appliance	BW Models																				
Triumph Vitesse Mk.2	EFE																				
Ford Capri	Lima																				
Triumph 2500	Springside																				
Mini Clubman	Springside																				
Austin Maxi	TPM (Projected model)																				
Leyland National Mk.I	EFE																				
Land Rover Series 3	Springside																				
Rover 2200	Springside																				
Bristol VR Series 3	EFE																				
Ford Capri Ghia	TPM																				
Leyland Olympian	EFE																				
Ford Escort	Springside, TPM																				
Volvo FL6 Fulton/Wylie Fire Appli	BW Models																				
Range Rover	Springside																				
Land Rover Discovery	BW Models																				
Volvo FL6/Dennis Fire Appliance	BW Models																				
Ford Transit Mk.3	Cararama																				

indicates a vehicle in production

indicates a vehicle no longer in production but still common on the road

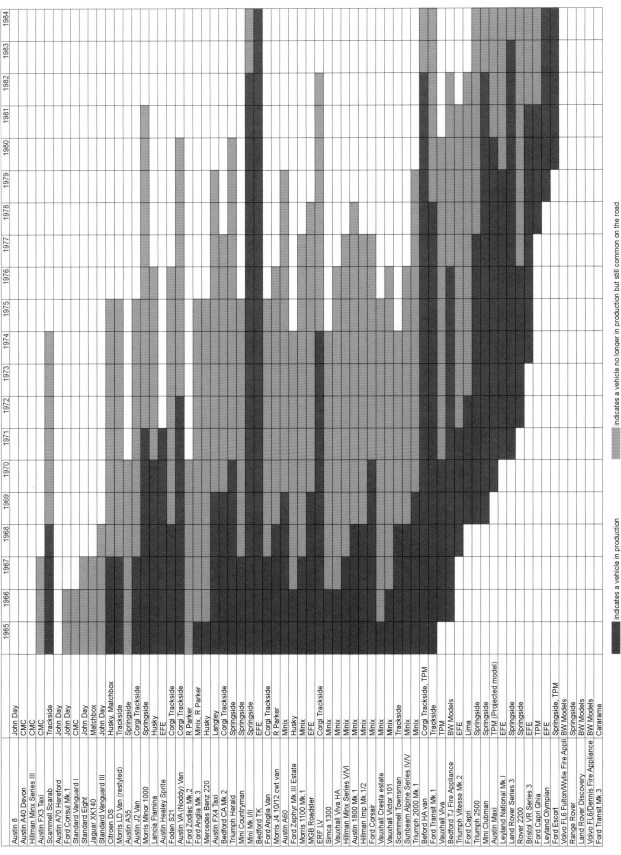

		1965	1966	1967	1968	1969	1970	1971	1972	1973	1974	1975	1976	1977	1978	1979	1980	1981	1982	1983	1984
Austin 8	John Day																				
Austin A40 Devon	CMC																				
Hillman Minx Series III	CMC																				
Austin FX3 Taxi	CMC																				
Scammell Scarab	Trackside																				
Austin A70 Hereford	John Day																				
Ford Consul Mk. 1	John Day																				
Standard Vanguard I	CMC																				
Standard Eight	John Day																				
Jaguar XK140	Matchbox																				
Standard Vanguard III	John Day																				
Citroen DS	Husky, Matchbox																				
Morris LD Van (restyled)	Trackside																				
Austin A35	Springside																				
Austin J2 Van	Corgi Trackside																				
Morris Minor 1000	Springside																				
Lancia Flamina	Husky																				
Austin Healey Sprite	EFE																				
Foden S21	Corgi Trackside																				
Austin VA (Noddy) Van	Corgi Trackside																				
Ford Zodiac Mk.2	R Parker																				
Ford Anglia Mk. 3	Minix, R Parker																				
Mercedes Benz 220	Husky																				
Austin FX4 Taxi	Langley																				
Bedford CA Mk. 2	Corgi Trackside																				
Triumph Herald	Springside																				
Mini Countryman	Springside																				
Mini Mk I/II	Springside																				
Bedford TK	EFE																				
Ford Anglia Van	Corgi Trackside																				
Morris J4 10/12 cwt van	R Parker																				
Austin A60	Minix																				
Ford Zephyr Mk. III Estate	Husky																				
Morris 1100 Mk.1	Minix																				
MGB Roadster	EFE																				
ERF LV	Corgi Trackside																				
Simca 1300	Minix																				
Vauxhall Viva HA	Minix																				
Hillman Minx Series V/VI	Minix																				
Austin 1800 Mk.1	Minix																				
Hillman Imp Mk.1/2	Minix																				
Ford Corsair	Minix																				
Vauxhall Cresta estate	Minix																				
Vauxhall Victor 101	Minix																				
Scammell Townsman	Trackside																				
Sunbeam Alpine Series IV/V	Minix																				
Triumph 2000 Mk.1	Minix																				
Beford HA van	Corgi Trackside, TPM																				
Ford Transit Mk.1	Trackside																				
Vauxhall Viva	TPM																				
Bedford TJ Fire Appliance	BW Models																				
Triumph Vitesse Mk 2	EFE																				
Ford Capri	Lima																				
Triumph 2500	Springside																				
Mini Clubman	Springside																				
Austin Maxi	TPM (Projected model)																				
Leyland National Mk.I	EFE																				
Land Rover Series 3	Springside																				
Rover 2200	Springside																				
Bristol VR Series 3	EFE																				
Ford Capri Ghia	TPM																				
Leyland Olympian	EFE																				
Ford Escort	Springside, TPM																				
Volvo FL6 Fulton/Wylie Fire Appli	BW Models																				
Range Rover	Springside																				
Land Rover Discovery	BW Models																				
Volvo FL6/Dennis Fire Appliance	BW Models																				
Ford Transit Mk.3	Cararama																				

■ indicates a vehicle in production   ▨ indicates a vehicle no longer in production but still common on the road

This appendix is a production-timeline chart. Models are listed with their manufacturer/range, plotted against the years 1985–2004.

Model	Range / Maker
Austin 8	John Day
Austin A40 Devon	CMC
Hillman Minx Series III	CMC
Austin FX3 Taxi	CMC
Scammell Scarab	Trackside
Austin A70 Hereford	John Day
Ford Consul Mk.1	John Day
Standard Vanguard I	CMC
Standard Eight	John Day
Jaguar XK140	Matchbox
Standard Vanguard III	John Day
Citroen DS	Husky, Matchbox
Morris LD Van (restyled)	Trackside
Austin A35	Springside
Austin J2 Van	Corgi Trackside
Morris Minor 1000	Springside
Lancia Flamina	Husky
Austin Healey Sprite	EFE
Foden S21	Corgi Trackside
Austin VA (Noddy) Van	Corgi Trackside
Ford Zodiac Mk.2	R Parker
Ford Anglia Mk.3	Minix, R Parker
Mercedes Benz 220	Husky
Austin FX4 Taxi	Langley
Bedford CA Mk.2	Corgi Trackside
Triumph Herald	Springside
Mini Countryman	Springside
Mini Mk.I/II	Springside
Bedford TK	EFE
Ford Anglia Van	Corgi Trackside
Morris J4 10/12 cwt van	R Parker
Austin A60	Minix
Ford Zephyr Mk.III Estate	Husky
Morris 1100 Mk.1	Minix
MGB Roadster	EFE
ERF LV	Corgi Trackside
Simca 1300	Minix
Vauxhall Viva HA	Minix
Hillman Minx Series V/VI	Minix
Austin 1800 Mk.1	Minix
Hillman Imp Mk.1/2	Minix
Ford Corsair	Minix
Vauxhall Cresta estate	Minix
Vauxhall Victor 101	Minix
Scammell Townsman	Trackside
Sunbeam Alpine Series IV/V	Minix
Triumph 2000 Mk.1	Minix
Bedford HA van	Corgi Trackside, TPM
Ford Transit Mk.1	Trackside
Vauxhall Viva	TPM
Bedford TJ Fire Appliance	BW Models
Triumph Vitesse Mk.2	EFE
Ford Capri	Lima
Triumph 2500	Springside
Mini Clubman	Springside
Austin Maxi	TPM (Projected model)
Leyland National Mk.I	EFE
Land Rover Series 3	Springside
Rover 2200	Springside
Bristol VR Series 3	EFE
Ford Capri Ghia	TPM
Leyland Olympian	EFE
Ford Escort	Springside, TPM
Volvo FL6 Fulton/Wylie Fire Appli	BW Models
Range Rover	Springside
Land Rover Discovery	BW Models
Volvo FL6/Dennis Fire Appliance	BW Models
Ford Transit Mk.3	Cararama

Year columns: 1985 | 1986 | 1987 | 1988 | 1989 | 1990 | 1991 | 1992 | 1993 | 1994 | 1995 | 1996 | 1997 | 1998 | 1999 | 2000 | 2001 | 2002 | 2003 | 2004

Legend:
- ■ indicates a vehicle in production
- ▧ indicates a vehicle no longer in production but still common on the road

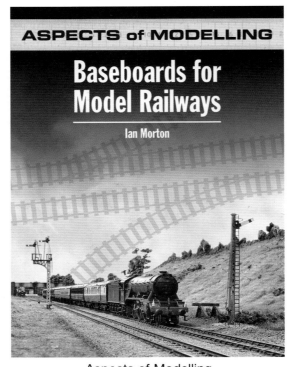